Still Interpreting
Vatican II

Still Interpreting Vatican II

Some Hermeneutical Principles

Ormond Rush

Paulist Press
New York/Mahwah, N.J.

Cover design by Sharyn Banks
Book design by Lynn Else

Library of Congress Cataloging-in-Publication Data

Rush, Ormond, 1950–
    Still interpreting Vatican II : some hermeneutical principles /
Ormond Rush.
        p.   cm.
    Includes bibliographical references and index.
    ISBN 0-8091-4285-6 (alk. paper)
    1. Vatican Council (2nd : 1962–1965). I. Title: Still interpreting
Vatican 2. II. Title: Still interpreting Vatican two. III. Title.

BX8301962 .R87 2004
262'.52—dc22

                                                            2004008869

Published by Paulist Press
997 Macarthur Boulevard
Mahwah, New Jersey 07430

www.paulistpress.com

Printed and bound in the
United States of America

CONTENTS

ACKNOWLEDGMENTS

I wish to acknowledge with gratitude those who generously read and commented on drafts of this book: Georg Denzler, Francis Schüssler Fiorenza, Tony Kelly, Richard Lennan, Greg Moses, John O'Malley, Otto Hermann Pesch, Michael Putney, and John Thornhill.

DEDICATION

I dedicate this book to my uncle Archbishop Francis Rush who, as a young bishop, attended all four sessions of Vatican II and who made the Council the lodestar of his episcopal ministry.

ABBREVIATIONS

AAS   *Acta Apostolicae Sedis*

The documents of Vatican II, the translations of which are taken from the Vatican's official version on its web site, are abbreviated as follows.

AA   *Apostolicam actuositatem*   Apostolate of Laity

AG   *Ad gentes*   Missions

DH   *Dignitatis humanae*   Religious freedom

DV   *Dei Verbum*   Divine Revelation

GS   *Gaudium et spes*   Pastoral Church in World

LG   *Lumen gentium*   Church Constitution

NA   *Nostra aetate*   Relationship w/ non-Christians

SC   *Sacrosanctum concilium*   Sacred Liturgy

UR   *Unitatis redintegratio*   Ecumenism

INTRODUCTION

Most of the bishops who attended Vatican II are sadly now dead. It is as if we have come to the end of some kind of "apostolic age"; "those who experienced it" have gone, and now it is up to those who follow to interpret and apply what they have written. Councils do not have an effect or impact on church life independently of the interpretative and applicative work of receivers who make the potentiality of the council a reality. *Effect* and *reception* go hand in hand; the history of a council's effect is at the same time a history of its reception.[1]

On the twentieth anniversary of Vatican II, Giuseppe Alberigo wrote: "Twenty years is too short a period for satisfactorily assessing the results of a great conciliar event."[2] Twenty years further on, we can say that *forty* years is still too short a period. But things may be a little clearer. "Truth is the daughter of time," wrote Newman;[3] "distanciation" is a good thing, according to Paul Ricoeur.[4]

On November 18, 1965, as the Council was coming to a close, Paul VI spoke to the assembly of a twofold task set for the church as it embarked upon its post-conciliar phase. "From now on," he said, "*aggiornamento* will mean for us an enlightened insight into the Council's spirit and a faithful application of the norms it has set forth in such a felicitous and holy manner."[5] Both (1) enlightened insight into the Council's spirit and (2) faithful application of the Council's norms are hermeneutical tasks. In this paper I wish to outline some hermeneutical principles that may aid the task of interpreting Vatican II forty years on.

There are two sets of triads that will be important as we progress through our inquiry. The first, from the discipline of philosophical hermeneutics, is the hermeneutical triad of understanding, interpretation, and application.[6] These three are inextricably linked but can be distinguished for the sake of methodological clarity. Briefly: we only ever come to *understanding* because we already have a framework of *interpretation* out of which we comprehend the meaning of some text or event or person; the new or unfamiliar is understood in terms of the old or the familiar. Therefore such an interpretative understanding is already an application to my present context. Understanding has taken place because I know what it means for me in my (albeit limited) horizon of experience; no one can force me to understand in *their* way. Thus, understanding, interpretation, and application are inextricably intertwined. That process necessarily takes place from horizons as diverse as the interpreters. In other words, if Vatican II is understood, interpreted, and applied, then that will be done, unavoidably, in a great diversity of ways.

The second triad, from the disciplines of literary and historical hermeneutics, is the triad of elements that make up any communicative event: (1) the original speaker or writer or author, (2) what is spoken or written or communicated, and (3) the addressee, the person who is spoken to or written to and who listens or reads or receives the communication. For our purposes, we will speak of these three elements as *author, text,* and *receiver.* The hermeneutics of reception I am proposing attempts to highlight the often-neglected third element, the reader or receiver, without forgetting the other two elements. Using the category of "reception," the "reception hermeneutics" outlined in this essay attempts to give equal weight to all three elements when interpreting Vatican II and its documents: the original event and the original authors, the documents themselves, and the people who after the event and the documents' promulgation attempt to understand, interpret, and apply them from the context of diverse cultures and contexts down through history after the event. I will name methodological attention to each of those three elements (1) a hermeneutics of the author, (2) a hermeneutics of the text, and (3) a hermeneutics of the receiver.

As we proceed to examine each of these elements, a further insight from the philosophical hermeneutical tradition will guide us, the notion of "the hermeneutical circle" (sometimes called "the hermeneutical spiral"). Briefly: understanding, interpretation, and application take place through a circular movement from "the whole" to "the part" and back to "the whole" again, in an ongoing circle of understanding. I understand a particular detail of a subject matter in terms of the overall view I already have; that new understanding of the particular, in turn, broadens my overall view. I understand "the part" in terms of "the whole," and vice versa. This back-and-forth process of questioning, from whole to part and back again, from general to particular and back again to general knowledge, is the rhythm of the hermeneutical circle or spiral. However, it is not a vicious circle; I don't just return to the same point in the circle. When I come back and take the helicopter view of the landscape, I understand it differently than before.

The principles outlined in this essay incorporate those philosophical, historical, and literary hermeneutical insights into a *theological* hermeneutics. Theological hermeneutics begins with the presumption of faith and the ecclesial context within which understanding, interpretation, and application of "the faith" take place. The hermeneutical circle, for example, is relevant to issues we will be addressing throughout this essay: tradition is to be interpreted in the light of scripture and vice versa; "the past" is to be interpreted in terms of "the present" and "the present" in terms of "the past"; Vatican I is to be interpreted in the light of Vatican II and vice versa; a part of a text is to be interpreted in the light of the whole text, and vice versa. This notion of the hermeneutical circle will be relevant also when we come to distinguish, without separating, notions such as "spirit"–"letter," "pastoral"–"doctrinal," "tradition"–"reception." And finally, the dynamic of the hermeneutical circle will be seen to apply to the methodological relationship between the three hermeneutical inquires of author, text, and reader; each is to be seen in the light of the other two, in an ongoing spiral of understanding.

1

A Hermeneutics

of the Authors

A hermeneutics of the author attempts to reconstruct the intention of the author or authors of a text. The meaning of Vatican II and its documents, for example, is here seen to lie in what the bishops wanted to communicate in the documents they promulgated; this "authorial intention" is reconstructed by examination of the pre-conciliar and conciliar proceedings over the four sessions and the intersessions. Reconstruction of this authorial intention constitutes a reconstruction of the so-called "mind" or "spirit" of the Council. As we will see, this historical reconstruction is the first, but not only, stage in the interpretation of the Council and its documents.

A hermeneutics focused on the authors looks to "the world behind the text" and the historical factors that conditioned its formulation.[1] The cluster of historical situations out of which the text emerges is here seen to be the initial primary guide when attempting to reconstruct what the text means. One of the major methods employed to retrieve that meaning could be broadly called the historical-critical method.[2] The meaning of the text, it is claimed, is to be found in what the authors intended it to say. Within a particular historical context, the bishops were attempting to formulate answers to questions arising out of that context. A historical reconstruction of those questions is important for interpreting the answers that were proposed to those questions. To understand the genesis of a text is to understand its meaning; therefore a historical reconstruction of the genesis of a text is fundamental for reconstructing the meaning of the text.[3]

Major studies have been carried out that attempt a hermeneutical reconstruction of the preparatory period, the debate and drafting regarding each of the documents, and the formation of a common mind among the participating bishops. The already-published four volumes of Guiseppe Alberigo and Joseph Komonchak's *The History of Vatican II* has become a significant resource for this stage of historical reconstruction of the world behind the texts.[4] Furthermore, more detailed analysis of the drafting of the four major constitutions is revealing the forces at work.[5]

Vatican II as an Event of Reception

Perhaps a helpful way of reconstructing the world behind the text and the intention of the bishops at Vatican II is to see the Council as an event of reception. The two terms require clarification.

I am using the term *event* here initially in a broad sense.[6] By "event" I mean the original historical gathering called Vatican II, from the calling of the Council by Pope John XXIII in 1959 and the preparatory period, the debates and voting on the Council floor during the four sessions (1962–1965), the informal interaction between bishops and theologians, the work of special commissions during the proceedings and the intersessions, up till the final public session on Tuesday, December 7, 1965, and the concluding ceremony the following day.

By "reception" I mean an interpreter's or group of interpreters' hermeneutical activity of making sense of people, events, traditions, or texts.[7] Reception is the assimilation and "making one's own" of another reality. This process of appropriation involves the interpreter in an active and creative way; the "effect" of past events or texts is determined to a certain degree on the active "reception" of a receiver. Reception includes judgments as to value and importance of some elements over others; it involves selection, that is, decisions to explicitly retrieve and foreground a particular dimension of the tradition and to allow another dimension to recede into the background. In this way, reception involves determinations of continuity and discontinuity. Thus a corollary of reception is nonreception; for example, what Vatican II did not receive from the past (or at least refigured differently in its new reception of the past by moving it to the background of its new Gestalt) is also important in interpreting its intention. The process of reception involves the dynamic of the hermeneutical triad and the hermeneutical circle; reception is the understanding, interpretation, and application of an event, a text, or symbol from the past from a particular perspective or horizon.

Vatican II was an event that can be understood as an attempt by the bishops to restate the church's self-understanding by re-interpreting the Catholic tradition in the light of contemporary challenges. Its reception of the tradition was multifaceted. The reality which it "received," in the above sense, was the living tradition, including the elements of scripture, doctrinal formulations, previous councils as events, the scholarly work of past and contemporary theologians, and so on. Ultimately, of course, the reality that it was receiving was what had been initially entrusted to the church: *revelation,* that is, the Gospel, the Christ event, God's self-communication and self-disclosure, God reaching out to humanity through Christ in the power of the Spirit. It had been from the beginning the mission of the church to tradition what it had received. Its reception, as evident by the plurality of christologies in the New Testament, had always found diverse expression throughout church history. Vatican II was now wanting to be faithful to its ecclesial mission: to constantly re-receive the Gospel in a new situation that required its rejuvenation.

Reception of the *Whole* Tradition

The genesis of Vatican II's documents could be said to have two historical phases: (1) that great sweep of church life throughout history, a living process of transmitting the Gospel, spanning from the Christ event right up to the calling of the Council in 1959, and (2) the preparation for and debate during the Council, including the drafting work of the various commissions. The prehistory of the Council is part of its history. But a further "nonecclesial" factor needs to be acknowledged as impacting on the Council: the world historical context in which the deliberations took place. Within the cultural, societal, and political shifts of the twentieth century, the 1960s were distinctive. Vatican II must be interpreted in the light of this wider context of world history. Therefore while a distinction can helpfully be made between "church history" and "world history," they constitute overlapping stories that impact each other.[8]

First, within the flow of church history, Vatican II is not to be interpreted as an isolated ecclesial event; it occurs within a living tradition as an attempt to re-receive that tradition in order to transmit it anew to future generations more effectively. It lies on a continuum of church life and is to be seen in continuity with all that has gone before. Within that living process of ecclesial reception and transmission, what is being retrieved from the past (then reconceived, and then passed on into the future) includes the myriad modes in which the church witnesses to the faith it has received: public and private prayer, especially the sacraments, scripture, creeds, doctrinal formulations, lives of the saints, writings of the patristic period, classic theological works, works of art, and so on, all forming part of a living process of traditioning "the faith" and applying it through Christian witness in daily life.[9] Vatican II is an event of reception of (within) that living tradition from a new horizon. It gathers the past into the present for the sake of a new future. The history behind the text therefore includes 2000 years of traditioning the Gospel leading up to the Council.

The slogans of *ressourcement* and *aggiornamento* marked this attempt to bring past tradition into the present.[10] It could be called a desire for a reception of the whole tradition.[11] Walter Kasper writes of the task of "extracting the council's intention....And this intention was the renewal of the whole tradition, and that means the renewal, for our time, of the whole of what is Catholic."[12] With perhaps an overemphasis on continuity in tradition, without regard for elements of discontinuity and innovation, the 1985 Extraordinary Synod, itself attempting a reception of Vatican II from a new perspective twenty years later, advanced a hermeneutical principle along similar lines:

> The Council must be understood in continuity with the great tradition of the Church and at the same time we must receive light from the Council's own doctrine for today's Church and the men of our time. The Church is one and the same throughout all the Councils.[13]

It has been a point often raised by Cardinal Joseph Ratzinger in his rejection of the notion that Vatican II constitutes a "break" or "rupture" in the continuity of church tradition:

> This schematism of a *before* and *after* in the history of the Church, wholly unjustified by the documents of Vatican II, which does nothing but reaffirm the continuity of Catholicism, must be decidedly opposed....There are no leaps in this history, there are no fractures, and there is no break in continuity. In no wise did the Council intend to introduce a temporal dichotomy in the Church.[14]

Leaving until later in this book discussion of Ratzinger's understanding of "continuity," it must be affirmed that the mind of the Council was certainly not to reject the past tradition, but to re-receive it into the present.[15] Otto Hermann Pesch formulates as a general rule for interpreting ecumenical councils: "No council is to be interpreted as fundamentally against the ecclesial tradition."[16]

However, reception of the past involves judgement and selection, where, for the sake of continuity of a greater tradition, certain elements of the past are deliberately placed in the background, or even rejected, in a new Gestalt of the great tradition.[17] While the word *change* is never used once in the Council documents, elements of newness and innovation abound. John O'Malley's hermeneutical rule is valid:

> While always keeping in mind the fundamental continuity in the great tradition of the church, interpreters must also take due account of how the council is discontinuous with previous practices, teachings and traditions.[18]

A distinction should be made, therefore, between "micro-ruptures" and "macro-ruptures" for the sake of a finer reconstruction of Vatican II's intention. Whatever of the micro-ruptures, whatever of the "innovations" and "discontinuities" that Vatican II introduced, the Council never intended a macro-rupture, never intended to sever itself from the great tradition; innovations and discontinuities (micro-ruptures) were seen to be ways of rejuvenating that broader tradition.[19] Such a broader perspective of the tradition would come through the *ressource-ment* program of the Council. Historical-critical methodologies would assist them in that search.

Reception of Historical-Critical Theological Scholarship

Highly significant for this reception of the great tradition was the openness on the part of the majority of the bishops to the shifting horizons of understanding and the emergence of new methodologies in Catholic theological scholarship of the mid-twentieth century. With a focus on *ressourcement* of the riches of the pre-Scholastic Catholic tradition, these approaches had come to be broadly characterised as the *nouvelle théologie*. In receiving the insights of these approaches, the Council was beginning the process of the Catholic Church's coming to grips with "history" as impacting its self-understanding and the very nature of its documents.

"Historical consciousness" had only become part of Western thinking with the emergence of the discipline of history, particularly in the nineteenth century. The importance of the impact of this consciousness on Vatican II was three-fold. First, it conditioned the Council's sense of itself as a historical event in a way that was not possible at any other council. Second, it came to a realization of "history," not only as an interpretation of the past, but as the present environment for proclaiming and living out the Gospel. Third, in terms of history as an interpretation of the past, historical consciousness impacted on the very approach to the documents and events of the past that it was seeking to retrieve and re-interpret.

In the first sense, Vatican II is unique among all the councils of the church in that it was explicitly conscious of its own place in history from the perspective of a historical consciousness.[20] There seems to be no doubt that the participating bishops were aware of the dramatic nature of what they were involved in and of what they were doing. They were making "history."[21]

In the second sense, "history as lived experience," the bishops were coming to grips with the relationship of faith and history.[22] It was to impact on their desire to link the doctrinal with the pastoral. Giuseppe Ruggieri sees this link as the major innovation of Vatican II:

> The main novelty of Vatican II was rather its consideration of history as related to the gospel and the Christian tradition. Whereas for the most part in the past there had been an awareness that history as experienced by human beings was ultimately of no importance for the understanding of the gospel (I use the term "awareness," although "in reality" it was never such a thing), the major question of the Second Vatican Council was precisely this, even if the words used (pastoral nature, aggiornamento, signs of the times) were not immediately understood clearly by all.[23]

This awareness will become particularly significant when we later come to assess the pastoral intention of John XXIII and the Council itself, its *aggiornamento* agenda, and its call for attention to the signs of the times.

In the third sense, "history" as "narrated history," the impact of historical-consciousness was channeled through the historical-critical methodologies employed by the theological *periti* who were on the various committees and who advised individual bishops or groups of bishops. In at least two ways, the *ressourcement* theologians brought historical consciousness to bear on the bishops' decisions. First, through their work, a broader notion of the Catholic tradition, beyond that of Medieval and Counter-Reformation Catholicism, was possible. There was "the greater and wider tradition, as distinct from its neo-scholastic levelling and simplification."[24] Second, the methods through which that past was retrieved were now historically critical. These new historical-critical methodologies were themselves the fruit of the emergence of a historical consciousness. What *Dei Verbum* taught concerning the appropriateness of a historical-critical approach to interpreting scripture (*DV*, 12) captures the approach that the Council was taking to its retrieval of the whole of the tradition.[25]

The issue of historical consciousness had emerged during the Modernist crisis and continued to dominate the agenda of theological inquiry in the half-century leading up to the Council. But shifts had been taking place. For example, despite Leo XIII's earlier attempt in 1879 to reinstate Thomism as a unifying factor for Catholicism,[26] there were cracks beginning to appear within neo-Scholasticism itself regarding the presumed unity of Thomism through a retrieval of a "Thomas before Thomism" by philosophers such as Henri Bouillard and theologians such as Marie-Dominique Chenu. Philosophers like Maurice Blondel and theologians like Henri de Lubac were moving away from extrinsicism to an immanentism in their conception of grace and nature, a shift that would have implications for modeling the relationship of the church to society and to the world. Evolutionary notions of nature and human psychology from nineteenth-century theologians like John Henry Newman and the

Catholic Tübingen school and from Pierre Teilhard de Chardin in the twentieth century were being received by theologians and were eventually received by the Council. The *communio* ecclesiologies of the early church and first millennium were rediscovered through the work of historical theologians like Yves Congar, ecclesiologies that contrasted with the later ecclesiologies of the second millennium. Possibilities of a different but genuinely Catholic conception of the church-state and church-society relationship, along with the question of religious freedom, were being retrieved by theologians such as John Courtney Murray.[27]

Therefore the Council is also an event of ecclesial reception of consensus in contemporary theological scholarship. Over four years of conciliar debate, there is evidence of an explicit widening of approach beyond the narrow perspective of the Counter-Reformation Catholicism and later neo-Scholastic frameworks, and a reception of the fruits of decades of research by biblical, patristic, liturgical, historical, and ecumenical *ressourcement* theologians. Vatican II's innovation was to break not only with the church's exclusive recourse to the neo-Scholastic framework and to embrace other methodologies, but also with the style of Catholicism that had surrounded the neo-Scholastic mentality. In this sense, it could also be described as a micro-rupture—a desire to break with the attitudes to theological scholarship characterizing the era of Pius X and the Modernist crisis.[28]

We cannot dwell too much on the individual contributions of the *periti* and members of commissions to the process of theological learning on the part of the bishops over the four years. Some of these theologians had previously been under suspicion in the era following the Modernist crisis. It could be said that Vatican II deliberately set out to portray a new model of mutual reception between magisterium and theologians. As an attempt at *aggiornamento* through *ressourcement* of the tradition, the Council's final documents were the result, in part, of a dialogue whereby at night bishops became learners and theologians the teachers, and by day the theologians listened as learners and the bishops once again assumed their teaching role.[29] In effect, this reception of contemporary scholarship was a reception of "history" in its broad sense.

Reception of Scripture and Other Elements of the Tradition

In Vatican II's reception of theological scholarship, in the service of its retrieval of the great tradition, several elements of that tradition (now interpreted with a greater historical consciousness) can be highlighted: scripture, the writings of the patristic period, the creeds and teachings of previous councils and popes, and the predominant theological framework of Thomism. Space permits only a few general comments; the issue of Thomism requires a more detailed examination.

In wanting to go back to the sources, the Council saw scripture as fundamental. It would capture this belief in its document on revelation: "[The church] has always maintained [the scriptures], and continues to do so, together with sacred tradition, as the supreme rule of faith" (*DV,* 21). Each page of the documents is dotted with references appealing to the witness of the biblical writings.[30] The gradual rejection of a neo-

Scholastic approach to proof-texting from scripture gives way to a rhetorical appeal to scripture as the primary witness to revelation. The labors of biblical scholars in the decades leading up to the Council were received into the discussion and helped shape the theological approach to the issue at hand.[31]

After scripture, particular pre-eminence is given to appeals to the patristic writers.[32] Attention to the footnotes of the documents reveals the importance for the Council of appealing to the patristic witness. Once again, the painstaking research of theologians such as Congar and de Lubac enabled that retrieval.

A further element in the Council's reception of the tradition is its reception of the decisions of previous councils, for example *Lumen gentium*, 51.[33] Of all the councils referred to in the footnotes of the documents, the previous two councils, Trent and Vatican I, make up half of all references to councils. The relationship between Vatican I and Vatican II is particularly problematic. According to Hermann Pottmeyer, "the central hermeneutical problem in the reception of Vatican II" is the question: "Is Vatican II to be read in the light of Vatican I, or is the direct opposite the case, or will the as yet unachieved reconciliation of the two councils show the necessity of a further stage in the development of ecclesial self-understanding?"[34] He goes on to propose the latter, that of a necessary new phase in its reception. That new phase would need to conceive of the relationship of the two councils in terms of a hermeneutical circle of understanding; Vatican II is to be understood in the light of Vatican I, and vice versa.

The reception of previous papal teaching is also an aspect of Vatican II as an event of reception of tradition. Of the recep-

Nothing in Vat II done in a Vacuum ->
hermeneutical circle

tion of previous papal teaching, references to Pius XII make up 50 percent. Alongside its retrieval of a broader tradition, the Council nevertheless wanted to weave tightly the threads of continuity with papal teaching of the immediate past.

Highly significant for reconstructing the "spirit" of the Council is the debate on the place of Thomas Aquinas in the Catholic tradition. Tracing the shifts in attitudes over the four sessions reveals a complex process of re-evaluating the place in the Catholic vision of what Leo XIII, in *Aeterni Patris,* had called "the perennial philosophy."[35] In the decades leading up to the Council, historical philosophers and theologians had been retrieving a Thomism before its neo-Scholastic versions.[36] But, paradoxically, this more historically rigorous retrieval resulted in a wide variety of contemporary Thomisms.[37] Such scholarship bore fruit during the Council's proceedings, in the twofold sense of having their *effect,* or impact, on the thinking of the Council and of their active *reception* and innovative assimilation in new ways by the Council. It was the first great surprise of the Council when, early in its proceedings, much of the work of the preparatory commission and the documents submitted for consideration in the first session were rejected. They had all been written from the perspective of the neo-Scholastic tradition predominant throughout the Catholic world and especially promoted by the Curia-led preparatory commission. The so-called "progressives" lined up in unity as a majority against the so-called "conservatives" presenting the neo-Scholastic line. The progressives were to win out. What was rejected was a framework that the majority considered a narrowing by neo-Scholastic theologians of the great Catholic tradition. What they now sought was retrieval of the wider Catholic tradition. But once unity had been achieved among the progressive majority concerning what was to be rejected, the problem then emerged: with what do we replace it?[38]

This problem becomes especially acute in the third and fourth sessions when two documents in particular come to be discussed: *Gaudium et spes* and *Dignitatis humanae*. The former unity of the "progressives" breaks down as they now begin to address issues such as the relationship between the church and society and the matter of religious freedom. Quite distinct theological anthropologies become apparent, which can be broadly described as "Augustinian" and "Thomist." The aula seemed to resemble a live pageant of Raphael's fresco *The School of Athens* adorning a wall in one of the old papal rooms in the Vatican Museum right next door to St Peter's Basilica: Plato is depicted pointing upward to a world of ideals and Aristotle alongside pointing downward to the world of concrete reality. The Augustinian school is wanting to set church and world in a situation of rivals; it sees the world in a negative light; evil and sin so abound in the world that the church should necessarily be always suspicious and distrustful of it. Any openness to the world would be "naïve optimism."[39] Theologians like Ratzinger and Henri de Lubac are the *periti* counseling bishops according to this model. The broadly named "Augustinianism" of this school seeks to bypass as illegitimate the great Medieval enterprise, even of a retrieved Thomas, and go "back to basics" to a scriptural and patristic version of the Catholic tradition. True to its "Platonic" orientation, here the doctrine of eschatology dominates, highlighting God's transcendence and the passing nature of this world.

The "Thomist" school is wanting to set church and world in a situation of dialogue; it sees the world in a positive light; despite evil and sin, grace abounds and will eventually overcome evil; attention to the "signs of the times" reveals new perspectives on God's salvific presence in the world here and now; the present redeeming activity in the world of the same God witnessed to in scripture provides the surest hermeneutical lens for interpreting faithfully those scriptures. Not a "naïve optimism" but a Christian realism urges an openness to the world as potentially revelatory. Theologians like Marie-Dominique Chenu, Karl Rahner, and Yves Congar are the *periti* counselling bishops according to this model. The Thomism of this school is that of the Aquinas retrieved by the *ressourcement* of historians of theology who had gone back to "the original Thomas," rejecting the departures from the master of his later interpreters. True to its "Aristotelian" orientation, in this school the doctrine of the Incarnation dominates, highlighting the goodness of the Creation within which the Son of God became incarnate.

Paradoxically, the formerly united progressive group of post-Scholastic Thomists, having rejected the Thomism of neo-Scholasticism, have now divided, forming two groups in the aula: (1) a new "progressive" group wanting to retrieve a re-interpreted Thomism and counseling openness to the world, and (2) a new "conservative" group wanting to retrieve the Augustinian vision and counseling caution in the church's relationship to the world.[40] In much the same way that the Renaissance saw the previous era as the dark "Middle Age" and desired to go back to the Golden Age of Graeco-Roman Antiquity as its exemplar, so too the new "conservatives" now saw the patristic age as the Golden Age of the church whose enterprise should now be emulated.[41]

Reception of Modernity and "the World"

This robust debate between the Augustinian and Thomistic theological anthropologies, each with their distinct visions of relating church and world, nevertheless finally resulted in the *commonly agreed vision* of the church in the world voted on in *Gaudium et spes* and *Dignitatis humanae,* both promulgated on December 7, 1965, the last day of the last session of the Council. It could be said that these two documents encapsulate the Council's eventual reception of modernity and of the world as necessary dialogue partners if the Gospel was to be preached in all its relevance. This openness (not outright acceptance) to modernity and to the world ended 150 years of suspicion, constituting a definitive "micro-rupture" with the official stance of the Pian era (from Pius IX to Pius XII). Rather than "naïve optimism," the documents exude an attitude of newfound Christian confidence and responsibility, replacing former fear and avoidance; rather than uncritical acceptance of the society and world around it, the documents demand critical application of one single and definitive criterion: Jesus Christ and the promotion of the reign of God.

In the shift to this new understanding of the church's relationship with the world, the bishops at Vatican II were not unaffected by the *Weltanschauung* of the society in which they lived and their responsibility in the face of the historical events that were going on around them. Reconstructive interpretations of the "history behind the text" must therefore attempt to situate the genesis of the Council documents within their historical context by considering world history though examination of the impact of contemporary events, culture, and *Zeitgeist.*[42] As has been said, "church history" and "world his-

17

tory" are overlapping stories and overlapping disciplines. In this way historians outline the diverse and indeed conflicting presuppositions the bishops might have had when they came to deliberate on the relationship between "church" and "world," particularly during the third and fourth sessions. They were reading the past from a particular historical time and context, each evaluating that time and context in diverse ways.

Therefore in the historical and theological reconstruction of this discussion, particular attention must be given to the church's former attitude to modernity in the 150 or so years that preceded the calling of the Council, from the French Revolution up until the calling of the Council in 1959. It is in this period that the peculiarly European form of the Catholicism that Vatican II set out to reform is fashioned. Although it is not "modern" in the sense of having a positive attitude to modernity, Komonchak names this form "modern Catholicism" to emphasis that, within the context of two thousand years of church history, it is a relatively late and recent form of Catholicism.[43] It is this peculiarly "modern" form of Catholicism that forms the backdrop for Vatican II's desire to restate its self-understanding with regard to society and the world. Could the Holy Spirit be providing them with resources from that very society for its task of rejuvenation of the tradition? Terms like *inculturation* and *contextualization* were about to be born.

"Modern Catholicism" had characterized contemporary society as tainted with the "liberalism" of "modernity"; its self-understanding was that of a *societas perfecta*, with its battlements constantly attacked by a godless, secular society. For a still Eurocentric church, the liberalism being condemned was the liberalism of post-Enlightenment Europe. According to Komonchak,

> The Second Vatican Council can be read as the event in which the Catholic church significantly reassessed modern society and culture and the attitudes and strategies it had adopted towards them in the previous century and a half. Those earlier attitudes and strategies had been founded in a consistent repudiation of an ideology and praxis summed up in the word 'liberalism.'[44]

Space does not permit a detailed analysis of the "liberalism" consistently denounced by popes throughout the nineteenth and twentieth centuries. The issue of the church's appropriate attitude in the face of such "liberalism," and whether it was the only tradition of liberalism available for their consideration, emerges with particular urgency during the conciliar discussion regarding religious freedom and the church in the contemporary world. Theologians like the American Jesuit John Courtney Murray were influential in presenting to the bishops an alternative tradition of liberalism that cohered with the Catholic tradition. It was this view that finally won out, ending with a rejection of the model of church as a *societas perfecta* and the embrace of a model that sees openness and dialogue with the world as essential to the mission of the church, and indeed as a mode of mission in the world.

Therefore in a striking micro-rupture with centuries of siege–mentality, the church opens the windows to modernity, now seen not so much as the enemy, but as a possible source of wisdom attuned to the Holy Spirit at work outside the boundaries of church.[45] But that micro-rupture was desired only for the sake of retrieving an approach to the mission of the church that was in *continuity* with the great tradition:

> From the beginning of her history [the church] has learned to express the message of Christ with the help of the ideas and terminology of various philosophers, and has tried to clarify it with their wisdom, too. Her purpose has been to adapt the Gospel to the grasp of all as well as to the needs of the learned, insofar as such was appropriate. Indeed this accommodated preaching of the revealed word ought to remain the law of all evangelization. (*GS*, 44)

Thus in *Gaudium et spes* 44 and 45 the Council recognizes what the church receives from the world, speaking of it in terms of reception—a living exchange *(vivum commercium)*.

Ironically, just as Roman Catholicism was receiving the elements of modernity judged to be consonant with the Gospel, Western society was entering the yet-to-be-named epoch of what is still vaguely called "post-modernity." Three years after the Council ended, the events of 1968 would shake the Western world. Furthermore, the forces of globalization would soon threaten the newfound appreciation of the local and the particular. As the insecurities of a post-modern era swept over the church, the context would be set for the reception of a Council that had only just begun receiving the now-ending "modernity," "by the skin of our teeth," as Kenneth Clark might have put it.[46]

Tentative Ecumenical Reception

It was the explicit intention of John XXIII that the Council be open to the perspectives of other churches and ecclesial communities for the sake of movement toward full communion. In effect, the Council tentatively recognizes that there have been authentic developments in the other ways of being Christian that have developed since the Reformation separation of the churches. This recognition is an acknowledgement that "the great tradition" could be received in a plurality of ways. The decades of work within the ecumenical movement were received by the Council and had their impact on the Council's vision.[47]

I do not need to elaborate on the extraordinary shift that Vatican II initiated toward reception of elements of the Christian tradition that had been previously considered "Protestant" and not "Catholic." Perhaps symbolic of the shift is the story of the pre-Reformation rector of the University of Prague, Jan Hus, who had sought many of the reforms that the later reformers would desire; he was burned at the stake on July 6, 1415, just down the road from where the Council of Constance was meeting. Vatican II, meeting 550 years later, in its document *Sacrosanctum concilium* n. 55, allowed communion under both kinds for the laity, something that Hus had been clamoring for and for which, among other things, he was condemned.

Another example of Vatican II's reception of a notion developed within Protestantism after the Reformation is the use by the Council of the trilogy "Priest, Prophet, and King" to structure *Lumen gentium* and to teach that the whole People of God participate in the threefold offices of Christ as

Priest, Prophet, and King, not just the hierarchy. Elsewhere I have written of this as a remarkable reception of a Protestant framework that had its origins in John Calvin and that had become a key notion in Protestant ecclesiology.[48]

Alongside the phenomenon of the Council's reception of particular elements of Protestant traditions into the Catholic tradition was the promulgation of the Decree on Ecumenism, *Unitatis redintegratio,* on November 21, 1964, setting the Catholic Church on a path of continuing dialogue with other Christian churches and ecclesial traditions for the sake of full communion. In this area alone, Vatican II must surely be regarded as a micro-rupture, *discontinuous* at least with the Catholic attitude of the previous four hundred years, and discontinuous with the previous two councils, all for the sake of a greater *continuity*—unity of ecclesial witness to the great apostolic tradition.

Conciliar Debate and "The Spirit of the Council"

The results of all these "receptions" come together and inform the work of the various commissions drafting documents and the discussion on the floor of the Council. Reconstruction of the history of the documents' formulation, as the Council attempted this multifaceted reception, provides the data for a reconstruction of what Paul VI called "the Council's spirit."[49] Pesch provides us with a helpful working definition:

The "spirit of the council" is the will of the over-whelming majority of the council Fathers which has emerged from the official record and in view of the pre-history of the council, even where it became watered down and weakened in particular by objections and sometimes unfair tricks of a small minority. As such it is a valid rule for interpretation of the conciliar texts....One can here truly say: The world-church stands behind this or that theological statement.[50]

If Kasper is right in asserting that "the council's inten-tion...was the renewal of the whole tradition, and that means the renewal, for our time, of the whole of what is Catholic,"[51] then "the spirit of the council" can be briefly summarized in the various slogans of "a new Pentecost," *ecclesia semper refor-manda, ressourcement* and *aggiornamento.*[52]

The notion of a reconstructed "mind" or "spirit" of the Council should not be understood in a historical-positivist sense. Nineteenth-century historical positivism claimed to be able to reconstruct "the" meaning of a past event or docu-ment as the authors explicitly intended. However, recon-struction of the "mind" of the Council is precisely that, a reconstruction. We have no direct access to some pure inten-tion of the bishops. We can only attempt to reconstruct *from our (shifting) perspectives* the meaning of their intention. Furthermore, such reconstruction of the spirit of the council is limited, since it is a historical-critical task that is always con-ditioned by the questions that the historian puts to the his-torical event from a new perspective; the answers to those questions are *interpretative reconstructions* by the inquiring

23

historian. For this reason alone, there is bound to be conflict of interpretations regarding faithful reconstruction of that "spirit." It is the thesis of this book that only hermeneutical consideration of each of the elements of author, text, and receiver will provide a balance of criteria for judging between conflicting interpretations.

Various interpreters have attempted a formulation of the mind or spirit of the Council. According to Rahner's reconstruction, it was the desire on the part of the bishops to become truly a world-church.[53] Kasper's basic interpretation of the Council, as we have seen, is that it desired nothing less than "the renewal of the whole tradition, and that means the renewal, for our time, of the whole of what is Catholic."[54] For Alberigo, the Council felt a "need of getting out of the post-Tridentine shoals, out of numbness and passivity."[55] O'Malley, in a more expansive articulation, has given his reconstruction of what he calls the "goals" or "aims" of the Council; he rejects minimalist interpretations of the Council for a view that sees the bishops explicitly intending to make a major turning point for reform in the history of Catholicism.[56]

Criticism of allegedly one-sided interpretations of the spirit of the Council has come from Ratzinger, who wishes to retrieve "the 'true' Council" by a "return to the authentic texts of the original Vatican II"[57] and to oppose reconstructions of the Council that, he claims, are in fact "a true 'anti-spirit' of the Council."[58] The key problem with this "pernicious anti-spirit," according to Ratzinger, is the claim that the Council marks a *rupture* with the past tradition, rather than an event in continuity with the tradition.

As noted above, it was clearly not the explicit intention of the bishops to break with the great tradition. But the issue remains as to how one conceives the role of innovation and discontinuity in the *preservation* of the living tradition of the church. Therefore, as I have suggested, a distinction must be made between a "macro-rupture" and a "micro-rupture," the former constituting a fundamental break with the great tradition and the latter constituting a break with a particular period or style within the tradition. In no way can the spirit of the Council be conceived as a desire for a macro-rupture with the tradition. However, a case can be made for the claims by various interpreters that Vatican II explicitly intended what I am calling certain micro-ruptures.

Various terms have been given by interpreters to the period or style that Vatican II is said to have broken from: *the Constantinian era, the Gregorian era, the Counter-Reformation era, the "modern Catholicism" of the Pian era.* Selected elements of discontinuity could be listed. Vatican II certainly broke with the Constantinian era through the Council's desire for dialogue with nonbelievers and in its rejection of the church-state. It certainly broke with the era of Gregory VII in its shift to a diversified world-church and its emphasis on collegiality. It certainly broke with the Counter-Reformation mentality through its appreciation of the independent reception of the great tradition by the separated churches. And it certainly broke with the style of modern Catholicism of the Pian era exemplified by the *Syllabus of Modern Errors,* of Pius IX, neo-Scholastic uniformity, and the authoritarian form of governance exhibited during the Modernist crisis and its aftermath. Philosophically, the Council can also be seen as a break with the uniform philosophical framework of a "Hellenistic Christianity" and as a shift toward the diverse catholicity of a world-church. The Council saw these breaks as *only* micro-ruptures, all for the sake of a return to the great tradition *(ressourcement)*, all for the sake of a way of being church that would be more effective in realizing the mission of the church in the world *(aggiornamento)*.

The (Holy) Spirit of the Council

The "spirit" of the Council can be understood in a double sense: (1) as the "mind" of the Council, and (2) as the "Holy Spirit," who, it was believed, was fashioning that common mind according to the mind of God. John XXIII had prayed for "a new Pentecost." Since the early councils there had been an enduring belief that the Holy Spirit would guide the deliberations of general councils. That conviction similarly drove the bishops of Vatican II. But it did not eliminate fierce debate and political intrigue.

Depending on how one conceives the dynamic of divine grace at work in human affairs, the debates and intrigue could very well read more like secular political history than an account of human beings imbued with ecclesial openness to the promptings of the Spirit. But those who hold that such intrigue means we should opt for a minimal interpretation perhaps have forgotten the similar plotting and lobbying seemingly evident at every other previous council. In response to Ratzinger's "minimal interpretation of the Council,"[59] one Australian bishop who attended all four sessions commented with the indignant riposte: "The Holy Spirit was there!"

But how did the Holy Spirit work at Vatican II? I will be arguing below that Vatican II, as "a new Pentecost," now requires of us a new pneumatology, that is, a new theology of how the Holy Spirit works.[60]

Method of Juxtaposition

How can one speak of a common "mind of the Council" or openness to the guidance of the one Holy Spirit amidst the political intrigue when there are clear compromises, ambiguities, and juxtaposition of conflicting viewpoints evident throughout the final documents? A few selective examples include: the notions of revelation in *Dei Verbum* and in *Nostra aetate;* the teaching of the Catholic Church as the sole bearer of truth and the recognition of elements of truth in the other Christian churches in *Unitatis redintegratio;* the repetition in *Lumen gentium* of Vatican I's teaching on the primacy of the pope and the affirmation of the equally supreme authority of the college of bishops.

The historian O'Malley calls the Council documents "committee documents, full of compromise and ambiguity."[61] Pottmeyer speaks of "the internal incoherence of the conciliar texts."[62] The conflicting camps or forces at work among the bishops remain encoded in the documents. Like the recurring battles in the history of literature between the *anciens* and the *modernes*,[63] the conservatives (the "ancients") and progressives (the "moderns") at the Council struggled to bridge the old and the new, continuity and innovation, sameness and difference, familiar tradition and unfamiliar signs of the times. Compromise and juxtaposition of viewpoints was the end result. Compromise and juxtaposition, however, did not necessarily indicate a lack of unanimity. Ecclesial unanimity was achieved at that particular time *through the retention of conflicting attitudes*. The fact remains that the final documents, despite all their ambiguity and conflicting positions side by side, were voted on and passed by the full authority of an ecumenical council as an ecclesial whole.[64]

Pesch's general hermeneutical principle reminds us that Vatican II was not unique in employing compromise statements: "With texts of the ecclesial magisterium one is always dealing with compromise formulae."[65] But Pesch claims that in the history of councils Vatican II is exceptional in its seemingly deliberate use of compromise as a way of maintaining what he calls a "contradictory pluralism."[66] He outlines two other types of compromise that had been evident in conciliar formulations of the past. First, a *Sachkompromiß* is an attempt to find compromise by stating the lowest common denominator on a particular matter of faith. He gives the examples of the creeds of the early church and, above all, the christological formula of Chalcedon. Second, a "dilatory compromise" is a compromise formulation that in fact defers a decision on a matter of faith because both positions are not contradictory but complementary. For example, Trent avoided canonizing either Scotist or Thomistic formulations. However, Vatican II's attempt at compromise is different, he claims. The compromise arrived at preserves a "contradictory pluralism" that deliberately sets in tension two positions, *leaving the issue open for future synthesis.*[67]

Where does this leave the interpreter? On the last day of the Council proceedings, Pope Paul VI addressed the assembly in his homily:

> Since the council had not intended to resolve all
> the problems raised, some were reserved for future
> study by the church, some were presented in
> restricted and general terms, and therefore they
> remain open to further and deeper understanding
> and a variety of applications.[68]

In other words, Vatican II hands over to future interpreters the
creative task of *reception,* that is, finishing off the job of arriving
at a new synthesis that could not be achieved at the time. What
was achieved was a juxtaposition of elements of the old with the
new. That, in itself, was a development. But "the needed synthesis is a task the Council sets for the Church and for theologians; it is a task of reception, which is far from being a merely
passive process."[69] The "spirit" of the Council was to leave
seemingly contradictory positions deliberately side by side.

   In our reception of their unfinished business, we therefore cannot simply return to the old debates on the Council
floor and choose one side or the other and continue to battle
it out, as is sometimes the case in the church today. A new
synthesis is demanded, keeping "the whole council"[70] in
mind. While Pottmeyer rejects interpretations that selectively
choose only one side or other of a compromise statement, he
emphasizes that the Council often gives a "stress" regarding
the two positions it has placed side by side:

> Fidelity to the Council also requires that we pay
> heed to the stress that the Council itself laid on the
> one or the other thesis, according as a thesis was
> supported by the majority or the minority. The fact
> remains, however, that majority and minority alike

agreed to both theses and in particular to their jux-taposition.[71]

While maintaining this stress, the new synthesis requires constant reconstruction of both "spirit" and "letter" throughout the ongoing history of the Council's post-conciliar reception.

Reception of the *Sensus Fidelium* and Pastoral Intention

John XXIII, in calling the Council and in his opening address, emphasized that the Council's focus should be pastoral, without separating the pastoral from the doctrinal.[72] Citing the prevailing negative attitude to surrounding culture and history in the 150 years preceding the Council, Giuseppe Ruggieri writes of John XXIII's vision in calling the Council:

> It is in this context that we need to see the significance of the key words of the magisterium of John XXIII. The category of the "signs of the times" is thus consistent with that of pastoral nature and *aggiornamento* and represents his own conception of Christian doctrine and the magisterium. Thus the signs of the times make it possible to rediscover the youth of the gospel, drawing from it, through the Spirit, *possibilities which earlier interpretations had not grasped....*History, not just of the past but above all of the present, with the vicissitudes experienced by men and women in our time, is a *locus theologicus.*[73]

This pastoral intention for the Council is evident, not only in the content of the final documents, but in the genre, style, and rhetoric of the final documents. They were explicitly not intended to be technical theological treatises. Rather they are often homiletic exhortations of pastors (much in the style of patristic homilies) that set out to appeal to the affective level of people's faith, indeed to appeal to any people of good will who would listen and respond.[74]

The pastoral focus on the part of the bishops was a deliberate intention to give attention to the *addressees* of revelation, the whole People of God. It became highly significant, for example, in the drafting of *Lumen gentium,* when the decision was made to place the chapter on the People of God before that on the hierarchy.[75] This pastoral attention to the addressees of revelation marks a shift to greater emphasis on the *sensus fidelium* as a source, criterion, and target of church teaching. It is the *universitas fidelium* who possess an infallibility in believing (in receiving revelation) on account of its anointing by the Holy Spirit (*LG,* 12).

The desire for a more effective application of the salvific Gospel in the daily lives of the faithful can be interpreted as an implicit desire to listen to the faithful regarding how the Gospel is indeed effectively transforming their lives. These are "signs of the times" requiring attentiveness, as the Council so strongly urged.[76] Open dialogue should not only characterize the attitude of the church to other Christian traditions, other religions and the world, but should also characterize the inner life of the church. The fruits of such intra-ecclesial dialogue could then, in turn, help the church speak and embody the Gospel more meaningfully and more truthfully. Greater attention to positive signs of the times paralleled a similar shift throughout the four sessions of the Council from a *deductive* methodology (formulating general axioms to apply to all situations) to an *inductive* methodology (examining particular pastoral cases first, and then formulating a general approach that might cover all cases).

The *pastoral* and the *doctrinal* aspects of the Council's teaching are therefore not to be set in opposition. The 1985 Synod formulated the appropriate heremeneutical principle: "It is not licit to separate the pastoral character from the doctrinal force of the documents."[77]

The Authoritative "Weight" of the Documents

The pastoral nature of the documents raises the issue of "canonical reception": various levels of authority claimed for church teachings demand appropriate levels of response by Catholics.[78] There are only two areas where the Council intended to define doctrine formally: the sacramentality of episcopal ordination and the matter of episcopal collegiality. However, even here, there has been conflict of interpretation. Francis Sullivan summarizes the mimimalist, maximalist, and moderate positions by various interpreters.[79] While the task of outlining the principles for "weighing" the authoritative nature of a particular teaching is different from the task of articulating the hermeneutical principles for interpreting what those teachings actually "mean," the interpreter must eventually give attention to both tasks.

In addition to the issue of formal definition of doctrine, it is clear that the Council intended to differentiate the authoritative levels of each of its documents by giving them different titles, although the precise authoritative significance of each title is never explained: "dogmatic constitution" (of which there are two), "pastoral constitution" (one), "constitution" (one), "decree" (nine), and "declaration" (three). Therefore when assessing the appropriate response required of the receiver, in terms of ecclesial assent, attention should be given to the different authoritative "weight" of each particular document and statements within those documents.

Inadequacy of a Hermeneutics of the Authors Alone

A reconstruction of the world behind the text and of "authorial intention" is not by itself sufficient for a full interpretation of Vatican II and its documents.[80] A historical-critical investigation of the genesis of the documents produces important guidelines for the interpretation of the Council. What the bishops intended, what political forces were at work in the process of drafting, the role of theologians, and particular theological methodologies are all important elements in reconstructing the intention of the authors. But such a historical reconstruction is always a retrospective reconstruction from a particular vantage point. Furthermore, such retrospective reconstructions change as historical perspectives change in time. The questions historians pose to the text change in the light of new contexts; these new questions are not necessarily illegitimate, despite the fact that they might not have been in the minds of the Council members.

There is no such thing as "the" meaning of a text, or "the" meaning of the Council (in a historical-positivist sense), and historians of the Council are unwise to pretend otherwise. Furthermore, there is more to the "meaning" of a text than what its authors explicitly intended to say. Future generations may find things in Vatican II that go beyond what the authors intended, but which are thoroughly in accord with the spirit and letter of the Council.

Vatican II shows the church taking on a historical consciousness. But, in the end, this historical consciousness was only in its infancy as a *modus cogitandi* regarding the church's self-understanding. The final documents exhibit a mix of two approaches, one historically conscious, the other ahistorical. However, it was a tentative start, one that would require further exploration in its post-conciliar reception, especially since the disciplines from which biblical and theological scholarship had learned the historical-critical method were themselves recognizing the limits of the historical-critical method and supplementing it with other methodologies, methods that focused on the *text* and the *receiver*. Post-modern theories of interpretation began to sound more like patristic and medieval methods of interpretation being retrieved by scholars such as de Lubac. Rather than trying to eliminate the strangeness of past texts through historical-critical reconstruction, post-modern theories began delighting in strangeness, "alterity," and "difference/deferring."

We have seen that reconstruction of the "spirit" of the Council is the task of a hermeneutics of the author. Attention to the "letter" is the task of a hermeneutics of the text. It is to that task that we now turn.

2

A Hermeneutics
of the Texts

A hermeneutics of the text takes the text "as is" and is not so much concerned about the debates and historical background that impacted on its formulation. If the previous approach was concerned about the "spirit" of the Council, this approach gives attention to the "letter." If the previous approach, in looking to the historical origins over time of the text, could be called a "diachronic" approach, this present focus on the text in its present form could be called a "synchronic" approach.

Across the hermeneutical disciplines, there are some, including theologians, who would want to promote an exclusive focus on a hermeneutics of the text ("the letter"). Structuralist theories in the 1960s and 1970s, for example, claimed the interpreter should forget about the original historical context of a text's production, and focus only on the text in its present state, in order to interpret its meaning. Once produced, it was claimed, the text is out of the hands of the author. Not only structuralists, but post-structuralists and deconstructionists, have proclaimed the death of the author; for some, the author's "codes" in the text are what guide meaning; for others, the infinite play between those codes means that there can be no limits to interpretation.

Such an extreme view takes things too far. Allowing an infinite play of the signifier has separated "letter" and "spirit." The author may be dead, but the author's words are there. It is a set text, and therefore sets limits to interpretation. A theory is needed that sees author, set text, and receivers in unending communication through time. But pushing a methodological "pause button" and focusing solely for the moment on the final and set text is legitimate.

Let us now briefly highlight some insights from this approach that can be helpful for interpreting Vatican II. Issues of genre, rhetoric, style, structure, intratexuality, and inter-textuality become important in the interpretative process.

Genre

The genre of Vatican II's documents is unique in the history of conciliar teaching. Pastoral in intent, the Council deliberately intended not to attack specific errors, but to renew the church in the light of urgent contemporary questions. Previous councils, in attacking specific errors, promulgated propositional statements, mainly in the form of "canons."[1] For such conciliar statements, there has developed an appropriate historical-critical hermeneutic.[2] Vatican II however promulgated no canons and deliberately set out to avoid a tone of condemnation of errors. "A peculiarity of Vatican II," asserts Rahner, is its "new mode of expression" through "instructions," or "appeals," which it employs in documents such as *Gaudium et spes*.[3] The interpreter should therefore give attention to this difference in genre of teaching. New hermeneutical principles apply for the interpretation of Vatican II. The genre of its documents and the tone of its language are like that of no council before it.

Rhetoric and Style

Closely related to the matter of genre is that of rhetoric and the tone of language adopted. The insights of rhetorical hermeneutics have recently emerged as a fruitful approach to the biblical text.[4] The application of these insights to doctrinal, and for our purposes, conciliar documents is only in its infancy. Gerard Hall has written on the importance of rhetorical devices for interpreting *Nostra aetate*.[5] O'Malley has likened the tone of the Council's documents to the style of discourse of Erasmus.[6]

As O'Malley has pointed out, it is methodologically unsound to apply a simplistic proof-texting approach to Vatican II documents, since it ignores the style or mode of expression in which the content is expressed:

> I must say that I continue to be surprised at how little study has been directed to the rhetoric of the Council, when we have learned over and over again that content cannot be divorced from style or literary form. If the style is the man, can we not assume, at least for the sake of discussion, that to some extent the style is the Council—and then by extension, that the style is the Church? If we wish to interpret the Council, we begin to pay attention

to this aspect of it, rather than focusing exclusively on the content proposed in certain documents or paragraphs. Here, if ever, proof-texting shows its well-known limitations.[7]

O'Malley's point regarding "the style is the Council" shows how important it is not to separate entirely examination of "letter" and "spirit," but to see them in a dynamic relationship, much like that of the hermeneutical circle.[8] Authorial intention can also be recovered in the style of communication; attention to the rhetoric of the "letter" can reveal the "spirit." O'Malley rightly points out that attention to the matter of how things are said is an important interpretative focus where the documents contain compromises and juxtaposition of seemingly contradictory views that can be selectively highlighted by one interpreter against another: "One problem with ignoring the style is that, because of its very discursiveness, somewhere in the documents of the council can be found a line to support almost every conceivable theological position."[9]

Does attention to the "letter" and "the authentic texts of the original Vatican II"[10] reveal no rupture with the tradition, as Ratzinger would claim? Or does attention to the style of the Council's "letter" indeed reveal that "Vatican II, for all its continuity in teaching with previous councils, was unique in its call for an across the board change in church procedures—or better, in church style"?[11] The Council may well speak of continuity in the "what" of being church; but does Vatican II constitute a definite break in the "how" of being church?

Here I believe it is possible to speak of a deliberately intended micro-rupture with other eras, particularly the ecclesial style of the Pian era (Pius IX–Pius XII). Not only in the rhetorical style, but also in the vocabulary of the Council, the letter reveals the spirit through its new "how" for church teaching—persuasion. This change is captured in the oft-repeated word *dialogue:* "For the first time in history, official ecclesiastical documents promoted respectful listening as the preferred mode of proceeding, as a new ecclesiastical 'way,' a new ecclesiastical style."[12] Collaboration rather than mere consultation, captured in Vatican II's teaching on "collegiality," although with deep roots in the history of the church, "indicates a break with the long-standing and then current style of ecclesiastical dealing."[13] The pastoral intention of the popes and bishops is therefore perhaps best exemplified in the challenge they set themselves: *to pastor in a new way.*

Structure

A few examples may sufficiently demonstrate the importance of structure in interpreting the meaning of single words, phrases, sentences, paragraphs, and chapters in the light of their place within a whole document. The structure of an earlier draft of *De Ecclesia* presented to the bishops had placed a chapter on the hierarchy before a chapter entitled "The People of God, and especially the Laity."[14] The final version of *Lumen gentium* has as its first two chapters "The Mystery of the Church" and "The People of God" (meaning pope and bishops, priests, deacons, religious, and laity) before going on to "The Hierarchical Constitution of the Church, Especially the Episcopate" and then "The Laity." This marks a significant shift from Vatican I, where the hierarchy are presented as the primary receivers of the Word of God who then pass it on to the rest of the church. Vatican II, however, teaches that the primary receiver of revelation is the whole People of God. According to this structure then, the teaching on the infallibility *in credendo* of the whole People of God (Chapter II, *LG*, 12) is treated before the teaching on the infallibility *in docendo* of the magisterium (Chapter III, *LG*, 25), indicating that the two forms of infallibility exist in a relationship of reciprocity, since what the whole People have received and believe must be what the church teaches.[15]

Attention to the structuring of a conciliar text in aid of its sound interpretation can at times also apply to individual sections of particular documents. One example is the structural analysis of *DV*, 12 by the biblical exegete Ignace de la Potterie. He demonstrates persuasively that the four subparagraphs have a chiasmic structure (A B B¹ A¹); attention to that structure aids interpretation of the whole paragraph.[16]

Intratextuality and Intertextuality

The focus here is on the meaning of a conciliar text in its "con-text," first its context within the whole document (synchronic issues of *intra*textuality) and, second, its context alongside other documents of Vatican II (synchronic and diachronic issues of *inter*textuality) and, indeed, alongside other texts of the past tradition to which they refer or allude (diachronic issues of *inter*textuality). A synchronic viewpoint examines relationships at the same time; a diachronic viewpoint examines relationship through time.

Principles of *intratextuality* remind us that words have meaning in the context of a whole work. The meaning of a word or phrase depends on its place in a sentence; a sentence is to be understood according to its place in a paragraph, a paragraph within the context of a chapter, and a chapter within the context of a whole document. This hermeneutical principle simply means that the interpretation of conciliar texts should follow normal lexical rules.

According to the principles of *intertextuality,* the immediate context of a single document is the whole "library" of documents that constitute the documents of Vatican II. Those texts, like the Bible, constitute a collection of texts sitting alongside one another. Once produced, they are to be seen not in isolation, but in terms of one another. The 1985 Synod notes this important hermeneutical principle:

> The theological interpretation of the conciliar doctrine must consider all the documents both in themselves and in their close interrelationship, so that the integral meaning of the Council's affirmations—often very complex—might be understood and expressed.[17]

But within that intertextual relationship, four documents, much like the hermeneutical function of the four Gospels within the whole Bible,[18] emerge as key hermeneutical points of reference. The 1985 Synod adds to the above hermeneutical principle of intertextuality: "Special attention must be paid to the four major Constitutions of the Council, which are the keys to the interpretation of the other Decrees and Declarations."[19] These four, of course, are, in chronological order of promulgation: *Sacrosanctum concilium* (December 4, 1963), *Lumen gentium* (November 21, 1964), *Dei*

Verbum (November 18, 1965), and *Gaudium et spes* (December 7, 1965).

Three important points need noting however, two of which are more canonical and theological than strictly related to a hermeneutics of the text per se. First, not all of those four documents have equal authoritative weight; two are titled "dogmatic constitutions," one a "constitution," and the last a "pastoral constitution."[20] Second, the later documents sometimes show development of teaching found in the earlier documents. Here a hermeneutics of the text must correlate with the insights of a hermeneutics of the authors. Over the four years, the bishops grew in understanding of the issues they were reflecting on, especially as they moved from discussion of the church *ad intra* to the church *ad extra*. Those later understandings should impact on our contemporary interpretations of the earlier documents. So just as the four Gospels are to be interpreted in the light of one another, so too the four major documents of Vatican II must be interpreted in the light of one another and the developing understanding expressed in each. And only then do they *together* constitute the hermeneutical key for interpreting the totality of the Council's library of documents. Third, according to the principle of the hierarchy of truths, *Dei Verbum* has a certain priority over the others, since one's notion of church *(LG)*, its worship *(SC)*, and its relationship to the world *(GS)* should derive from the prior notion of how one conceives God's revelation and its reception-transmission in history.

When confronting the Council's problematic practice of juxtaposing viewpoints in tension, the interpreter is confronted with issues of intertextuality. One example is the tension in Vatican II's teaching regarding revelation and its transmission. Rahner has pointed out that *Dei Verbum* (promulgated November 18, 1965) assumes that revelation begins with Abraham, and "does not exactly present a concept of 'revelation' which is easily accessible to African and Asian cultures, particularly since the millennia between 'primitive revelation' and Abraham remain unfilled."[21] However, he notes, in *Nostra aetate* (promulgated three weeks earlier on October 28, 1965) one finds that "for the first time in the history of the Church's teaching, the way was prepared for a positive appraisal of the great world-religions."[22] He further notes that *Lumen gentium, Ad gentes* and *Gaudium et spes* teach the universal salvific will of God, which only an individual's conscience can thwart; here, Rahner claims, "an opportunity of really salvific faith in revelation is admitted even outside Christian verbal revelation."[23] *Dei Verbum* therefore, although promulgating teaching regarding a "higher" doctrine according to the hierarchy of truths, must be interpreted (re-interpreted) in the light of the other documents.

Likewise Pottmeyer notes that the Council's reception of a wider (and more ancient) notion of a "living tradition" impacted on the developing ecclesiology of *Lumen gentium*. *Dei Verbum* and *Lumen gentium* therefore are to be seen as mutually interpreting one another. He writes:

> At this point the intrinsic connection between the "Constitution on Revelation" and the "Constitution on the Church" becomes visible: the advance in ecclesiology is supported by the way in which the "Constitution on Revelation" relates sacred scripture and tradition to each other.[24]

The principle of intertextuality therefore is not unrelated to the historical-critical issues that emerge in reconstructing the intention of the authors; in other words, the hermeneutics of the text must return at some stage to the hermeneutics of the author. Of particular significance for interpretation of the "letter" of the Council is the fact that learning and broadening of horizons were going on in the minds of the bishops during those four years. That developing "mind" or "spirit" must impact on the interpretation of the "letter."

Therefore is it legitimate that the later *Gaudium et spes* (promulgated December 7, 1965) should function as a lens for the interpretation of the earlier *Lumen gentium* (November 21, 1964)? O'Malley, for one, calls *Gaudium et spes* "a long and extremely important codicil to *Lumen gentium*."[25] Ratzinger, on the other hand, believes that it is illegitimate to consider *Gaudium et spes* a more mature document than the earlier *Lumen gentium*.

> Are we, then, to interpret the whole Council as a progressive movement that led step by step from a beginning that, in the "Dogmatic Constitution of the Church," was only just emerging from traditionalism to the "Pastoral Constitution" and its complementary texts on religious liberty and openness to other world religions—an interpretation that makes these texts, too, become signposts pointing to an extended evolution that will permit no dallying but requires a tenacious pursuit of the direction the Council has finally discovered? Or are we to regard the Council texts as a whole in which the documents of the last phase, which are directed

to the Church's relationships ad extra, are, n
theless, oriented toward the true center of faith
that is expressed in the dogmatic constitutions on
the Church and on divine revelation? Are we to
read the dogmatic constitutions as the guiding
principle of the pastoral constitution, or have even
the dogmatic pronouncements been turned in a
new direction?[26]

Instead of Ratzinger's stark either-or choice between the
approach that highlights the development that took place
between the two documents and the call to consider the
conciliar texts as an interrelated whole, attention to the
whole Council requires an approach of "both-and." His
seemingly exclusive synchronic approach to "the authentic
texts of the original Vatican II," and the methodological
exclusion of any development in the bishops' thinking as
relevant to a reconstruction of the true "letter" and "spirit"
of the Council, privileges a static notion of "letter" and
ignores the importance of ongoing learning on the part of
the bishops for a reconstruction of the "spirit" of the
Council. We have already seen the dynamic at work when,
as bishops and theologians interacted over the four years,
the bishops by night became the learners and the theologians the teachers, and the theologians by day became the
learners and the bishops the teachers, once they re-entered
the aula. Vatican II's own notion of the progress of tradition
in *DV,* 8 well describes the ecclesial process of learning taking place over the four years of the council.[27] Furthermore,
while Ratzinger rightly emphasizes that *Lumen gentium* is a
dogmatic constitution and that *Gaudium et spes* is only a

pastoral constitution, such a principle for weighing the relative authority of the documents requires, however, the supplementary hermeneutical principle enunciated by the 1985 Synod of Bishops and mentioned above:

> The theological interpretation of the conciliar doctrine must consider *all the documents both in themselves and in their close interrelationship,* so that the integral meaning of the Council's affirmations— often very complex—might be understood and expressed.[28]

That interrelationship and that complexity requires that diachronic attention be given to the *developing* self-understanding as a church that took place when the bishops moved from having considered *ad intra* issues in *Sacrosanctum concilium* (liturgy) and *Lumen gentium* (the church) to addressing the issue of the church *ad extra* in *Nostra aetate* (on the relation of the church to non-Christian religions), *Dignitatis humanae* (on religious liberty), and *Gaudium et spes* (on the relation of the church to the world). Only a hermeneutics that gives attention to both diachronic and synchronic issues by interrelating a hermeneutics of the authors and a hermeneutics of the text will do justice to the complexity highlighted by the 1985 Synod and will achieve a mutually critical relationship between "spirit" and "letter." One could well appropriate Pottmeyer's statement quoted above to the relationship between *Gaudium et spes* and *Lumen gentium:* "At this point the intrinsic connection between the 'Pastoral Constitution on the Church in the Contemporary World' and the 'Constitution on the Church' becomes visible: the advance in ecclesiology is supported by the way in which the 'Constitution on the Church in the Contemporary World' relates church and world to each other." After the Council, the issue of ecclesial dialogue *ad intra* will emerge as an unresolved issue during the period of the Council's reception.

The principle of intertextuality extends discussion beyond a consideration of the Council's own documents to a consideration of their reference to a whole network of other Christian texts from the great tradition, including scripture, creeds, teachings of previous councils and popes, as well as theological, spiritual, and liturgical texts. This diachronic extension of "context" in ever-widening concentric circles overlaps with the notion of the Council as an event of reception of the great tradition, an issue we have already examined above.

The evidence within the conciliar texts of this intertextual linking among other texts of the great tradition is similar to a dynamic evident in the history of literature highlighted in recent decades by literary theorists.[29] Authors allude to authors alluding to authors. Individual texts seem to lack any meaning that can be said to be independent of the matrix of texts that have preceded them. One can say of Vatican II's reading of the tradition what Graham Allen says of the dynamic between literary texts:

> Reading thus becomes a process of moving between texts. Meaning becomes something which exists between a text and all the other texts to which it refers and relates, moving out from the independent text into a network of textual relations. The text becomes the intertext.[30]

If Adso, William of Baskerville's companion in Umberto Eco's novel *The Name of the Rose*, were to wander through the "library" of books that are the documents of Vatican II, his discovery might well be the same as when he wanders through the labyrinthine library of the novel:

> Until then I had thought each book spoke of the things, human or divine, that lie outside of books. Now I realized that not infrequently books speak of books: it is as if they spoke among themselves. In the light of this reflection, the library seemed all the more disturbing to me. It was then the place of a long, centuries-old murmuring, an imperceptible dialogue between one parchment and another, a living thing, a receptacle of powers not to be ruled by a human mind, a treasure of secrets emanated by many minds, surviving the death of those who had produced them or had been their conveyors.[31]

A living tradition, indeed! A glance through the footnotes of any edition of Vatican II's documents reveals something of the network of *explicit* intertextual referencing. It would be a worthy edition of those documents that had also in the margins the list of texts of the tradition each particular line might be alluding to *implicitly*. The "letter" of Vatican II is not a dead text, but a long, centuries-old murmuring, an imperceptible dialogue, a living thing, one point in the continuum of the great tradition.

Spirit and Letter

Already I have noted that a hermeneutical focus on the text does not mean that we are attempting to see the "letter" of the text completely in isolation. Reconstruction of the "spirit" of the Council and of the "letter" of the Council texts are two points on a hermeneutical circle of inquiry. The 1985 Extraordinary Synod emphasizes that "it is not legitimate to separate the "spirit" from the "letter" of the Council."[32] The principle that spirit and letter are to be mutually informative highlights the need to distinguish, but not separate, the task of reconstructing the world behind the text from the task of reconstructing the world of the text. They are to be distinguished only for the sake of methodological clarity.

O'Malley, we have seen, notes that "the style is the Council" and urges the avoidance of such a concentration on the "letter" that it ends up being "proof-texting," "focusing exclusively on the content proposed in certain documents or paragraphs," while ignoring the way in which the content is expressed.[33] Thus attention to *the way in which the letter is expressed* is an important element in keeping "spirit" and "letter" in relationship; "letter" is to "spirit" as content is to style. Interpretation of "the spirit of the Council" (what the Council intended) and interpretation of "the letter" (the texts of the Council) are interrelated tasks. They exist in the relationship of a hermeneutical circle. Pottmeyer describes that circle:

> Despite the limitation [of not going beyond juxtaposition of theses] of the conciliar texts, the "spirit" of the Council is tied to them, because

without them it would lack any sense of direction. The "spirit" of the Council makes itself known from the direction given in the texts. Conversely, of course, it is only in this "spirit" that the texts are properly understood.[34]

Interpretation of the texts reveals the "spirit"; the "spirit" guides the interpretation of the texts.

The Implied Readers

One particular problem when taking an intertextual approach to the documents (as a way of keeping "spirit" and "letter" in creative tension) is the breadth of concern of the bishops. According to O'Malley, "among the elements that make Vatican II unique in the history of ecumenical councils is the scope of its concerns and the scope of the persons it addressed."[35] Throughout the documents, the intended receivers named include Catholics, sometimes "the People of God," and sometimes "persons of good will." *Gaudium et spes,* for example, is not only addressed to Roman Catholics, but rather is addressed to "the whole of humanity" (*GS,* 2).

This notion of the texts' addressees becomes more concretized as we now move from the texts' "implied readers" to a hermeneutics of the real receivers—those real flesh-and-blood interpreters who have received these documents over the last forty years.

Inadequacy of a Hermeneutics of the Texts Alone

Just as the previous focus on the history of the text's formulation alone was inadequate, so too an approach that focuses solely on the documents alone is inadequate. The documents cannot be totally divorced from the event that gave rise to them. A hermeneutics of the authors and a hermeneutics of the texts must therefore be two complementary approaches. The second builds on and attempts to complement the previous historical approach's attempt to get behind the world of the text and to trace the text's genesis.

However, even bringing these two approaches into a complementary relationship is still insufficient.[36] There is a further element that needs to complete the picture for a comprehensive hermeneutics for conciliar texts. And that element is the receiver of the documents: the one who takes them up and reads them, and attempts to understand, interpret, and apply them. What is needed to balance both a hermeneutics of the authors and a hermeneutics of the texts is a hermeneutics of the receivers.

3

A HERMENEUTICS
OF THE RECEIVERS

Interpretation of the meaning of Vatican II and its documents does not end with a historical reconstruction centered on those four years in the early 1960s. Nor does it end with a textual examination of its documents. The last forty years have now become part of the meaning of the Council. The history of the Council includes the history of its reception. Indeed, the historical meaning, or significance, of Vatican II in the sweep of church history is now dependent on those who receive it and will (or will not) make it significant.[1] As Kasper states it:

> Whether this council will count in the end as one of the highlights of church history will depend on the people who translate its words into terms of real life. What is at issue for Catholic theology, therefore, is not the council in itself. What is in question is the interpretation and reception of the council. The dispute is about this and this alone.[2]

Likewise, Ratzinger highlights the importance of post-conciliar reception by the whole church in the determination of a Council's effectiveness:

A Hermeneutics of the Receivers

While the Council formulated its pronouncements
with the fullness of power that resides in it, its historical significance will be determined by the process
of clarification and elimination that takes place subsequently in the life of the Church. In this way, the
whole Church participates in the Council; it does
not come to an end in the assembly of bishops.[3]

The receivers of Vatican II will determine its place in history. Who are those receivers? Just as *LG*, 12 states that the primary receiver of revelation is the whole People of God, so too,
in the interpretation of the Council, the same theological truth
applies. The whole People of God is the primary receiver and
interpreter of the Council. As Alberigo writes:

> Only the *sensus fidei* of the Church as a whole can be
> the adequate interpreter of a major council. Such a
> *sensus fidei* can reach maturity only slowly, with the
> concurrence of the entire people of God; it cannot
> be replaced by an action of the hierarchy alone.[4]

How is this "*sensus fidei* of the Church as a whole" to be discerned? If we accept Rahner's basic theological interpretation
of Vatican II as a shift from a Eurocentric church to the
notion of a truly world-church,[5] the issue of multiple *loci
receptionis* will become critical in discerning the *sensus fidei* of
the world-church as a whole.

The very category "reception" has only recently been
retrieved. Jean-Marie Tillard called it "certainly one of the most
important theological re-discoveries of our century."[6] It was
long an axiom of medieval scholasticism: *Quidquid recipitur*

ad modum recipientis recipitur (That which is received is received in the mode of the receiver.) The calling of Vatican II stimulated ecumenical research into the principle of conciliarity in the early church.[7] The reality of "reception" quickly emerged from that research as a striking characteristic of ecclesial life in the first millennium. It was noted, particularly in seminal studies in the early 1970s by Alois Grillmeier and Congar,[8] that what happened after a council was also a part of that council's history. A council's reception was recognized as significant in judging its effectiveness, and therefore its meaning, as a historical event.[9] Furthermore, beyond emphasizing the need to examine the post-conciliar life of a council's decrees within a local church, they note that a dynamic of reception between local churches constituted a fundamental feature of being church in the first millennium when an ecclesiology of *communio* was predominant; the church understood itself as a *communio* of churches. In the second millennium, they note that a *communio* ecclesiology shifted to a more hierarchical notion of church, with a consequent downplaying of the ecclesial dynamic of *communio* and *receptio* between local churches.

Grillmeier elsewhere highlights the kerygmatic, theological, and spiritual dimensions of post-conciliar reception.[10] For our purposes, the distinction is helpful. On the *kerygmatic* level of formal promulgation of official teaching, issues of "reception" relate to whether such teaching is accepted (or not) within a local church or between local churches. A lot of discussion today simplistically reduces reception to only this sense: reception or non-reception understood as acceptance or rejection. *Theological* reception refers to ongoing reflection on the subject matter of the conciliar teaching by theologians in the local churches. *Spiritual* reception refers to the assimilation by the faithful of a council's teaching, applying it to their daily lives. In all three dimensions one can speak of *hermeneutical* reception. Whether it be acceptance of a formal promulgation, theological reflection, or spiritual appropriation of the council, the hermeneutical triad of understanding, interpretation, and application is always involved. Hermeneutical reception of Vatican II, therefore, is the process within the receiver(s), from the perspective of their particular context, of attempting to understand, interpret, and apply the Council and its documents.

According to a hermeneutics of reception, a text is dead until it is read. Vatican II is not achieved until it is received. The documents are dead until they are read ("read" in the sense of understood, interpreted, and applied). It is the receiver who brings the documents to realization. That process requires that the receiver *make* sense of them; it requires that they not only find meaning but also *give* meaning to them. The original authors (the bishops of Vatican II) require involvement by the receiver(s) of the Council for communication of meaning to be realized. In that sense, the receiver is a co-creator of the meaning of what is communicated.[11] Hence that appropriated meaning could legitimately go beyond original authorial intention. Ricoeur speaks of a text's "surplus of meaning."[12] With multiple contexts from which a text may be interpreted, the original authors "need" future readers to make sense of a text whose authors may not have had those future contexts in mind.

Many factors come to bear on the reception process of making new meaning: class, gender, race, culture, geography, and local history, to name just a few. Typically, hermeneutical reception is always a selective process; one reader may bring to the fore as highly relevant something that another reader leaves to the background as not as relevant to his or her context. Furthermore, distanciation and a retrospective view on an event can provide new insights. A retrospective view of an event's meaning years later can find new meanings beyond those envisaged by the protagonists at the time. For example, from the perspective of the participants, the Congress of Versailles marked the end of World War I. In retrospect, it marks the beginning of the path toward World War II, with the stringent conditions it laid upon Germany.[13] Is a similar negative assessment valid for Vatican II?

All of this has relevance for understanding the reception of Vatican II over the last forty years. The particularities that have characterized the diverse reading communities of the Council have been almost numberless. Perhaps this has been one of the most significant learnings of these forty years. We have come to a greater realization that *perspective*—whether it be class, gender, race, culture, geography, or local history—conditions any process of interpretation. Context and *locus,* where the receiver is situated, condition reception and the way particular communities make meaning, make sense of the Council and its documents. Consequently, there have been multiple *loci receptionis* of the Council.[14] Yet again, Rahner's thesis was correct. Once the local and the particular are given their ecclesiological significance, the hermeneutical significance of the local and particular can likewise be highlighted, as a reception hermeneutics aims to do.

The phenomenon of multiple *loci receptionis* in the church at any one time is the *synchronic* dimension of reception. It highlights the diversity of *local* churches throughout the world church receiving documents from the *universal* magisterium.[15] Only a few representative works can be cited of authors who have written on this synchronic aspect of the Council's reception.[16] Gilles Routhier has written on the reception by the Archdiocese of Québec in Canada.[17] Adrian Hastings has written of the reception by local churches of Africa.[18] David Pascoe in his doctoral work has examined the reception of Vatican II by local churches in Australia.[19] A number of Latin American theologians can be noted. Leonardo Boff sees the Council as both a point of arrival and a point of departure. As a point of departure it opened up opportunities for creative reception, going beyond what the original authors could have envisaged, but, according to Boff, in fidelity to the spirit of their reforms:

> The Second Vatican Council had an enormous impact on the Latin American Church. The spirit of the Council, together with its corpus of documents, wrought two decisive effects here. First, a church renewal already well on its way now enjoyed official legitimation. Second, now it would be possible to implement a creative acceptance of the Council from a point of departure different from that of the Council's own conception, realization and development: the point of departure being the viewpoint of the poor.[20]

Other Latin Americans have written on the reception of the Council, for instance, Segundo Galilea[21] and Gustavo Gutiérrez.[22] Therefore, despite the fact that Vatican II gave insufficient attention to the socio-economic situation of oppression of the majority of Catholics throughout the world, there has been a remarkable reception of Vatican II by liberation theologians. More research is needed on the reception of the Council from the perspective of gender, race, culture, geography, or local history. However, according to some interpreters, it is this very diversity of receptions that constitutes the basic problem in the history of the Council's reception: "it is not Vatican II and its documents...that are problematic [rather] the manifold interpretations of those documents which have led to many abuses in the post-conciliar period."[23]

Within a decade of the Council's close, conflicting evaluations in terms of achievements and abuses in the Council's reception soon became apparent throughout the world. According to Joseph Komonchak, three general positions are discernible.[24] The "progressive" interpretation, sharply contrasting pre- and post-conciliar Catholicism, sees the Council as rejecting what had gone before and lays the blame of the problematic reception of the Council on restorationist forces, particularly from the Roman Curia. The "traditionalist" interpretation, also depicting the Council as a rupture, sees that rupture as a betrayal of the Catholic past. Archbishop Marcel Lefebvre exemplifies this position. Komonchak then notes a third, "mediating" position. This so-called middle position, professed by Ratzinger, is suspicious of any appeal to the "spirit" of the Council that is not grounded in the "letter" of the documents themselves. For this position, the Council was not a rupture with the past, but stands in full continuity with the Catholic tradition; any talk of discontinuity is not grounded in the texts themselves, but rather in a going-beyond of the clear intention of the Council to perpetuate the great tradition. Since the "traditionalist" group rejects the Council outright, contemporary discussion on the reception of the Council has focused on the two groups that Komonchak would typify as "progressive" and "mediating."

Both of these groups have legitimate criticisms of the other. Among both progressive and mediating proponents there have no doubt been "abuses" of the Council, going beyond the intention of the Council through a selective reading of its "letter." Among some progressives, that selectivity has gone beyond even the constraints of the selected texts, leading to what can legitimately be called "abuses" of the Council, with vague appeal to the spirit of the Council. Among some proposing the mediating position, there has been a clear intention to roll back the micro-ruptures that the bishops intended, going beyond the Council by an equally selective reading of its "letter."

It can be claimed that such selectivity has marked the official reception of the Council by the Roman Curia. Many feel that, in recent decades, the Curia has continued to operate under the shadow of its former head Cardinal Alfredo Ottaviani, with his motto of *Semper Idem,* by downplaying the deliberate micro-rupture with the Pian era intended by the Council and by continuing on its curial style as if the Council had never happened. Therefore those claiming the mediating position, while accusing the progressives of abuses and of going beyond "the true council," are not wholly innocent of wanting to go beyond the Council themselves. In accusing the Council itself of aping the "naïve optimism" of "the Kennedy era," and undermining its true identity by being critical of its own past, Ratzinger writes:

> The kind of self-accusation at which the Council
> arrived with respect to the Church's own history

was not sufficiently aware of this fact and so expressed itself in ways that can only be called neurotic. It was both necessary and good for the Council to put an end to the false forms of the Church's glorification of self on earth and, by suppressing her compulsive tendency to defend her past history, to eliminate her false justification of self. But it is time now to reawaken our joy in the reality of an unbroken community of faith in Jesus Christ. We must rediscover that luminous trail that is the history of the saints and of the beautiful—a history in which the joy of the gospel has been irrefutably expressed throughout the centuries.[25]

Perhaps to describe the history of the church as "that luminous trail that is the history of the saints and of the beautiful" itself sounds very much like the "naïve optimism" of the Kennedy years, and itself requires correcting in its view of church through the same dark, pessimistic glasses through which the Augustinian school looks so suspiciously upon the world.

These tensions came to the fore at the 1985 Synod of Bishops meeting twenty years after the close of the Council. It met to assess the reception of the Council. Avery Dulles has characterized the three very different theological mindsets that were apparent during the Synod discussions as the "neo-Augustinians," the "communitarians," and the "liberationists."[26] The last, however, was not a dominant group at the Synod. Dulles's characterization of the two dominant "schools" could very well make a neat characterization of the division in the debate twenty years earlier over *Gaudium et spes* and *Dignitatis humanae*. The neo-Augustinians, as described by Dulles, tended to separate church and world, highlighted the "mystery" of God and the church, accented worship, were eschatologically focused and otherworldly. The communitarian school (with many of the characteristics of the Thomist school at the Council) saw the church involved in the world working for its transformation, highlighted "communio" over "mystery," were optimistic in their assessment of secular society, highlighted the Incarnation as the model for the church's embrace of the world, and were thus "this worldly" rather than otherworldly.

Almost twenty years after the Synod, this typology is still helpful in naming the conflict of interpretations of the Council. Komonchak writes:

> It would be an interesting study to compare, without simplifying things, the interpretations and evaluations of the Council and especially the post-conciliar decades given by Thomistically inclined and trained theologians to those given by theologians whose intellectual affections move more spontaneously in the direction of the Bible and the Fathers, especially Augustine.[27]

It has been noted that during the third and fourth sessions, there was a divide across the aula floor during the *Dignitatis humanae* and *Gaudium et spes* debates. The voices of Augustine and Thomas, at times with the accent of Plato and Aristotle, could be heard speaking through the interventions of certain bishops. This same typology of positions continues to characterize the reception of the Council. For Komonchak, the two major types are "Augustinian" and

"Thomist." Just as the image of the Raphael School of Athens can be applied to the later sessions of Vatican II, the same image can now be applied to the reception of the Council.[28]

The "Augustinian" reception of the Council can be loosely described as lying within the philosophical tradition of Plato (and its later Augustinian reception). Its proponents, some of whom were among the "progressives" in the first two sessions of the Council who rejected the dominance of neo-Scholasticism in the draft documents, were now wanting, seemingly, to throw out the Thomist baby with the neo-Scholastic bathwater. Theologians like Ratzinger and Henri de Lubac now looked back, beyond the medieval Thomistic achievement, to the great Golden Age of the Fathers, especially Augustine.[29] Like the Renaissance thinkers of an earlier cultural revival who looked back past the Middle Ages to the great Golden Age of the ancient Greeks and Romans, these post-conciliar interpreters of Vatican II now bypassed Thomas for the great Christian antiquity of the biblical and patristic eras.

The "Thomist" ("communitarian") reception of the Council can be loosely described as lying within the philosophical tradition of Aristotle (and its later Thomist reception). Its proponents, some of whom were likewise among the "progressives" in the first two sessions of the Council who rejected the dominance of neo-Scholasticism in the drafts, were now wanting to build on the Thomist vision as still appropriate for capturing the peculiarly Catholic vision concerning the sacramentality of all Creation. Optimism was at the heart of a Catholic confidence that God will reign; the Incarnation has brought about redemption of a fallen world.[30] These scholars, far from wanting to give hermeneutical privilege to one particular period in the great tradition, sought also to incorporate the riches of the biblical and patristic revivals of *ressourcement* theology, as the work of a Congar or a Rahner attest. The style of this Thomist reception is perhaps best characterized by the approach of the Dominican Chenu, who looked to the "real" Aquinas in a retrieval that emphasized the positive value of Creation because of the Incarnation.[31]

Who is right and who is wrong? A pessimistic reading or an optimistic one? Is it legitimate to employ, as a hermeneutical guide for judging conflicting interpretations of the Council, John XXIII's deliberate intention to make a break with "prophets of doom"? In appeals to tradition, how is tradition to be conceived, and what is the role of innovation and discontinuity in that traditioning process? What criteria of fidelity do we have to make such judgments about conflicting interpretations of the tradition? Does the patristic period display a greater fidelity to the Gospel than does the medieval achievement? Is it a matter merely of "intellectual affections" among theologians for one theological tradition over the other, or is one more faithful to revelation than the other?

These are among the major questions that demand common ground from the conflicting interpreters of the Council. I can only make three points: (1) the way forward will not be found in returning to the positions taken up on the Council floor and found juxtaposed in the texts; (2) criteria of interpretation must be faithful to the theological epistemology of Vatican II itself; and (3) the ecumenical dialogues that have been a fruit of the Council may perhaps supply the Catholic Church with a methodology that will enable it to go beyond the conflicting interpretatio its own communion.

First, in what Grillmeier would call the "theological reception" of a Council, the way forward will not be found by taking
sides in the Augustinian-Thomist debates that were going on
during the Council, but rather by an attempt to move on from
the deliberate compromise and juxtaposition of approaches to *a
new synthesis,* as demanded by the Council.[32] Just as the problem
of Vatican II's juxtaposition of theses should not be resolved
through some "selective interpretation—'conservative' or 'progressive,' depending on the viewpoint of the interpreter—that
seizes upon one thesis in a pair without attending to the other
and incorporates it into a given line of argument,"[33] so too the
current impasse in the interpretation of Vatican II will not be
overcome through a selective interpretation that chooses either
the Platonic/Augustinian or the Aristotelian/Thomist lines of
thought in the documents. Returning to the Augustinian-
Thomist debate is a dead-end street; new synthesis is what is
required. At the very least, that synthesis would want to main-
tain as necessary the tension between the concerns of both the
Augustinian perspective and the Thomist perspective. Both are
vital shades in a full depiction of "the great tradition," and like
the chiaroscuro of a Rembrandt painting, together they repre-
sent the living tradition in all its darkness and light, with all its
pessimism and optimism, suspicion and trust: forever suspicious
of what could impede the reign of God, yet never losing hope
that God will certainly reign in the end-time, and firmly believing that God is active in hidden ways in the world today, even
in the seemingly godless, as attention to the signs of the times
would verify.

But, after Vatican II, a new Catholic synthesis, incorporating the strengths of both the Augustinian and Thomist
lines of the great tradition, can no longer be a return to the

totalizing syntheses of the past, nor a synthesis where, through some monologic Hegelian dialectic, opposition and difference are overcome and eliminated. Furthermore, a new unified Catholic vision in the spirit of Vatican II will be a synthesis that maintains Catholic unity in Catholic diversity by highlighting that it is only through the multiple *loci receptionis* of the one Gospel throughout a world church that the church fulfils its mission. The *sensus fidelium* at work incarnating the Gospel in these multiple *loci receptionis* needs to be valued as a crucial criterion for interpreting revelation, alongside the work of theologians and the magisterium. And a new Catholic synthesis after Vatican II will be one that emphasizes church as humble servant to the reign of God. We have already noted that, in Dulles's typology of schools of thought at the 1985 Synod, the "liberationist" school was dominated by the "neo-Augustinian" and "communitarian" schools. Will it be the liberationist school that will show us the way forward to a new Catholic synthesis where church relates to the world with an Augustinian suspicion well too aware of evil's ways, but with a Thomist confidence that the church, as mere servant to a world where God will surely reign, can help transform the ways of human living according to the image of the One who became human like us? Such is the task of ongoing reception of the Council.

Second, what is needed in that ongoing reception is a theological epistemology according to the Council's own teaching. *Dei Verbum* provides the Magna Carta for such an epistemology. Revelation is here portrayed, not only as truths about God and human living, but fundamentally as God's loving self-communication to humanity though Christ in the

ˈthe Holy Spirit. Tradition is accordingly portrayed not simply as a collection of traditions, but as a living process in which the church offers to the whole world the opportunity of responding in loving faith to God's outreach to humanity through Christ in the power of the Spirit. This is "the great *traditio*," the deposit of faith, the great treasure given to the church in trust. All else is in service of that mission.

Dei Verbum speaks of five witnesses to salvific revelation: scripture, tradition, magisterium, theology, and *sensus fidelium* (correlating *DV* 8 and *LG* 12). Although each is a distinctive authority in its own way, a theological epistemology faithful to Vatican II will always depict all five witnesses as necessary, mutually critical criteria for judging faithful receptions of revelation (God's self-communication through Jesus Christ in the Spirit).[34] All five witnesses, the Council teaches, are assisted by the Holy Spirit. In the theological reception of Vatican II, one of the most urgent tasks that the Council has left theologians is the task of developing a new theology of the *sensus fidelium*, the long-underplayed fifth criterion.

In other words, the reception of Vatican II itself cannot take place in isolation from the ongoing reception of these five witnesses to revelation. Indeed, the event of the Council and its teaching have now become part of the patrimony of church tradition, along with all other councils. It is to be judged in terms of its capacity to effect "the great *traditio*": God's offer of salvation through Christ in the Spirit. Vatican II is to be assessed over time by its effectiveness in achieving greater adherence to Christ and transformation of the world in his image. Attention to the *diachronic* dimension of reception sets out to trace the history of the Council's reception through time as the *synchronic* receptions from diverse *loci receptionis* continue. Vatican II lies along a continuum of two thousand years of church history and becomes a historical event that itself undergoes a process of reception.[35] Just as Vatican II was an event where a re-reception of scripture and tradition took place, so too the reception of Vatican II itself is now *only one element* (albeit an important hermeneutical key) in the church's wider ongoing reception of revelation (the Gospel witnessed to in scripture and tradition). Its authority as a council is demonstrated to the degree that it effectively facilitates, through reception of its "spirit" and "letter," that wider ongoing reception of the Gospel.

Third, in the application of that theological epistemology, what method can help us through the current impasse of conflicting interpretations of Vatican II? Perhaps an answer is to be found in one of the great fruits of the Council, the ecumenical dialogues with separated churches and ecclesial communities. Over the last forty years, a consensus is emerging as to how best to proceed in ecumenical dialogue. It has been found that a "comparative method," whereby contradictory positions were explained and justified, was not bearing fruit. In recent decades, there has emerged what is called an "ecumenical methodology."[36] Instead of comparing and contrasting traditions, both parties attempt to interpret together the apostolic tradition. If each can recognize in the other's interpretation "the apostolic faith," then surprising agreement and common ground can be achieved. If this ecumenical methodology were to be applied today within the Catholic Church, in a common reception of the unified diversity of the apostolic tradition by all groups, then the way forward may be opened to a new synthesis.

Until now, in outlining a reception hermeneutics, I have been employing "reception" as an investigative principle. With its focus on the receiver of a text, reception hermeneutics has provided principles related to the investigation of the Council's history of reception. I now also wish to suggest that the category of "reception" can provide a structuring or integrating principle for a theology of the Council's "Spirit."

4

A NEW PENTECOST:
A NEW PNEUMATOLOGY

I spoke above of the importance of the receiver's creative involvement in bringing any text alive, at times finding meanings beyond authorial intention, and I have claimed that this is not only unavoidable in the reception of Vatican II, but is necessary for its "spirit" and "letter" to be balanced in diverse reception contexts. The "spirit" of the Council's *aggiornamento* reform agenda demands similar creativity in its reception. "What was written with imagination must be read with imagination."[1] The "spirit" of the Council demands it; the "Spirit" of the Council *enables* it. But the Council's "spirit" demands that we conceive a new way of modeling how the enabling of the "Spirit" actually works. A new Pentecost demands a new pneumatology. It must be a pneumatology of reception and could appropriately be called a pneumatology "from below." I will call it a "reception pneumatology."

Can the category of "reception" provide a structuring principle for an integrated christology, pneumatology, and Trinitarian theology, and therefore, ecclesiology? A sketch of a proposal can only be given here. God the Father gives of himself to humanity through Jesus Christ. The Father is, at once, the Giver of God's self-communication and the

Receiver of Christ's self-gift to the Father in return. Jesus Christ is, at once, humanity's reception of God and God's reception of humanity. The Holy Spirit is the *dynamis* of giving *(traditio)* and receiving *(receptio)* between Father and Son, and between the Triune God and humanity. The Holy Spirit is the Spirit of Reception not only between Father and Son, but also the Spirit of Reception between the Triune God and humanity. *Communio* in the Trinity is therefore an active process of *receptio* within the Trinity. Humanity's invitation to *communio* with God is an invitation to participate in the dynamic of *receptio* within God. It is the Holy Spirit who facilitates this active "participation" *(koinonia, communio),* what St. Paul called "the *koinonia* of the Holy Spirit" (2 Cor 13:13). In the process of divine communication within God, the Holy Spirit is the Dialogue between Father and Son. In the process of divine self-communication between the Triune God and humanity, the Holy Spirit is the Dialogue who enables response to God's Address to humanity and whose way is the way of dialogue. It is on this trinitarian foundation that the ecclesial principle of synodality or conciliarity rests, since the church is called to be an icon of the Trinity. In enabling faithful interpretation of revelation (God's self-communication through Jesus Christ in the Spirit), the Holy Spirit works in human affairs through reception and dialogue.

Since the early church there has abided the belief in the assurance of the Holy Spirit's assistance for maintaining *continuity* with the tradition whenever bishops meet in council.[2] *The same Holy Spirit at work during a council is at work in the history of reception of that council and its documents.* Here a principle that Vatican II enunciated for the interpretation of *scriptural* texts can be applied analogically to *conciliar* texts. *DV*, 12, paragraph C, speaks of the need for an ecclesial reading of scripture.[3] It states that "Holy Scripture must be read and interpreted in the sacred spirit in which it was written." "Spirit" here, asserts de la Potterie, is to be understood pneumatologically.[4] The same Spirit who inspired the individuals and communities, whose faith the biblical texts witness to, is also at work through the history of the church, enlightening (inspiring?) reading communities to understand the meaning of the biblical text for their time and place. So too, the same Spirit who assisted the bishops at Vatican II in their reception of the tradition assists the reception by the *universitas fidelium* of Vatican II and its documents in the light of the "Spirit" of the Council,[5] achieving what Paul VI wished for, "an *enlightened* insight into the Council's spirit."[6]

The document *Dei Verbum,* in paragraph 8, speaks of an assurance of the Holy Spirit's guidance in relation to the transmission of revelation down through history. "This tradition which comes from the Apostles develops in the Church with the help of the Holy Spirit. For there is a growth in the understanding of the realities and the words which have been handed down" (*DV*, 8b). It then goes on to state how this help of the Spirit is communicated. Three means are named: the *sensus fidelium,* the work of theologians, and the oversight of the magisterium, in that order.[7] All three are named as instruments of the Holy Spirit.

Throughout the four years of conciliar debate, there was a growing pneumatological awareness among the bishops.[8] That growth in awareness within the church has not stopped developing since the Council. Congar makes an important point that is relevant to present reception of the Council:

> Pneumatology, like ecclesiology and theology as a whole, can only develop fully on the basis of what is experienced and realized in the life of the Church. In this sphere, theory is to a great extent dependent on praxis. Paul VI brought to a close the Council inaugurated by John XXIII and repeated his predecessor's desire for a new Pentecost. Some years after the close of the Council [1973], he was able to say: "The Christology and especially the ecclesiology of the Second Vatican Council should be followed by a new study and a new cult of the Holy Spirit, as an indispensable complement of the conciliar teaching."[9]

In other words, that "new Pentecost" now requires a new pneumatology. The Council had only begun to initiate a whole revision of what it means for the Holy Spirit to guide the church through history. It had only just begun to grapple with history itself!

The rise of historical consciousness had a significant impact on the desire for reform among the bishops at Vatican II, as we saw in the section on the hermeneutics of the author. But, as O'Malley points out, there were different styles of historical thinking operating on the Council floor and evident in the final documents.[10] These styles are not mutually exclusive, and sometimes elements of one style are evident in another.

The first style, or model, is that of "substantialism" or "essentialism." This has been the dominant classic model in

Roman Catholicism. John XXIII articulates it in his "sub-stance/expression" model during the opening speech: "The substance of the ancient doctrine of the deposit of faith is one thing, and the way in which it is presented is another."[11] This model sees realities such as "revelation" or "church" in terms of the same substance that endures through history and is unchanged by history. This same substance, like a Platonic ideal, is said to assume different forms, or expressions, in dif-ferent times and cultures. The second model O'Malley notes is that of "providentialism." What God wants to happen is all laid out in the eternal past. Here God is understood as an agent in human history bringing about the predefined divine purpose. The Holy Spirit is portrayed as an agent of Divine Providence, fashioning the processes of human minds and decision-making according to that eternal and fixed plan. The contingencies of human history do not change God's original intention. If any change of the divine plan is envisaged, it is termed "emendation," as John XXIII calls it in his opening address. The third model is what could be called "exemplar-ism." The past, as history, helps us in the present by provid-ing exemplary models for us to emulate. Our task is to do what they did.

These three models of historical thinking emphasize *con-tinuity*, but don't envisage any *discontinuity* throughout his-tory. The fourth model does. It is the model of "primitivism." This model, according to O'Malley, envisages some ideal period of the past that was a Golden Age that needs to be recre-ated because of the perceived decline subsequently away from that ideal. Whether it be the time of Jesus, or those first years of the post-resurrectional community in Jerusalem, or the patristic age, or the Middle Ages, or even better, Catholicism of the 1950s in Brisbane or Sydney or Melbourne, this style of historical thinking sees reform as a return to that so-called perfect time when all was well, and if only we could recreate that Golden Age, all would be well again. Slogans like "rejuvenation," "revival," "rebirth," and perhaps even the word "reform" itself, all are rally cries to "get back."

An interesting subset of "primitivism," O'Malley notes, is the reversal of looking *back* to the past and, instead, looking *forward* to the future in search of that Golden Age when all *will* be well. Influenced by the Enlightenment notion of "progress" and nineteenth-century models of evolution, theological theories of organic evolution and development are here employed to explain the task of reform in the church: the church began as a seed that we must nourish so that it can develop into what it was originally genetically encoded to become in the distant future.

O'Malley, while accepting the insight of each of the four models, proposes that they are inadequate for understanding the radical notion of reform that Vatican II quite deliberately but inchoately was proposing, despite instances of all four models throughout the final documents. The main difficulty he sees is that they don't cope with *discontinuity* along with continuity, and all have a benign notion of tradition without sufficient suspicion of the past. "What all these 'philosophies of history' have in common is that they are traditional or conservative as regards the past."[12]

Contrary to Ratzinger's rejection of "rupture" theories of any kind, a careful interpretation of the "spirit" of the Council, I believe, along with O'Malley and others, reveals a radical intention on the part of the bishops. According to

Komonchak, a retrospective interpretation of the
along the continuum of church history does indeed show that
it constitutes an "event," in that it marks a radical break beginning a new epoch.[13] Retrospectively, and seen within the context of two thousand years of church history, the Council can
now be seen to constitute a deliberate break with particular
elements of the tradition (variously named Constantinian,
Gregorian, Counter-Reformation, Pian, etc.), now judged to
be impeding continuity with the great tradition and impeding
a more effective *receptio/traditio* of the Gospel in the contemporary world. This radical intention I have named in terms of
a desire for micro-ruptures from those elements.

O'Malley and Komonchak highlight that a philosophy
and a theology of history are now needed in the light of that
radical intention, one that brings to the fore the discontinuity
(albeit in terms of micro-ruptures) that the Council itself introduced as necessary for faithful continuity with the past. As
noted already, I believe there is a need for a new pneumatology
to accompany that new theology of history, a new theology of
the Person of the Holy Spirit and of how the Holy Spirit works
in human history. A pneumatology of *aggiornamento* is needed
that incorporates discontinuity along with continuity.

The model of ecclesial reform that I am proposing sees
reform as "constant re-reception," effected in the Spirit. Such
a reception model of reform highlights the creative involvement with God on the part of the receivers of revelation, that
is, the creative involvement of human beings in the decisions
of history and in the creative interpretation of "what God
would want" the church of the future to be. The new
Pentecost Vatican II desired requires a reception pneumatol-

ogy. Rather than seeing God and God's Spirit as intervening in human consciousness, canceling human freedom, and eradicating any human processes of creativity and decision-making, the human receivers of revelation are to be portrayed as active participants in discerning the way forward, co-deciders with God's Spirit, assuring continuity through creative discontinuity.

There is no distillable fixed "eternal divine plan" for the church that is to be divined (beyond the God fully revealed in Jesus Christ), as the model of "essentialism" would propose. There is no interventionist God mechanically manipulating the will and decision-making of human agents on the stage of human history, as "providentialism" would propose. There are no exemplars from the past who can adequately model for us appropriate responses to the new and unique problems that history has thrown before the world of the twenty-first century, as "exemplarism" would propose. And there is no Golden Age, either in the past or in the future, that can be so finely described as to constitute a divinely given blueprint that neatly fits the unique and multiple situations that local churches find themselves in as "primitivism" would propose. What *has* been given as the ultimate criterion, the *regula fidei,* is the life, death, and resurrection of Jesus Christ, which must be received over and over in the power of that Spirit who "will guide you into all the truth" (John 16:13).

Vatican II reveals the church coming to a realization that, in response to the task given by our God, *it is up to us to work it out as we go along*—with the help of the Holy Spirit whispering through all the criteria for fidelity and continuity supplied by interrelating the five witnesses to revelation (scripture, tradition, *sensus fidelium,* theology, and the magisterium).

There is no essence, no mechanically intervening God, no perfect exemplars, no ideal age, that allows us to avoid the
responsibility of struggling to understand, interpret, and apply
the Gospel anew in a thousand new situations. However,
although it is our responsibility, *it is not our work*. It is the
work of the Holy Spirit, who is our communal memory, pre-
venting ecclesial amnesia and igniting our creativity.[14]

That creative Spirit who hovered over the chaos, that
creative Spirit who came on prophets and on Jesus himself,
who came upon the first Christian communities to guide
them in their adaptation of the Gospel as they moved out of
Palestine to a Hellenistic world, who came upon those communities as they gathered and sorted their foundational documents as the new Christian Scriptures, who came upon the
318 bishops at Nicaea in 325 as they struggled to sort out
Arius, that same Holy Spirit is urging us on, like a director
offstage, whispering into our ecclesial ear, not telling us
exactly what to do, but bringing us together in council (ecumenical, regional, national, diocesan, parish, or otherwise) *to
dialogue about it*. That sevenfold insistence of the writer of
the Book of Revelations, "Let anyone who has an ear listen to
what the Spirit is saying to the churches" (Rev 2:7, 11, 17,
29; 3:6, 13, 22), may sound suspiciously like "providentialism," with the Spirit revealing some predetermined plan to
the churches of Asia Minor. However, one day I am sure they
are going to find, hidden in a craggy corner of Nag
Hammadi, a text that reveals what the Spirit may have been
saying to those churches. And it may have been: "What do
you think we should do?"

Luke in Acts has Paul saying in the letter sent out to the churches after the so-called Council of Jerusalem: "*It has seemed good to the Holy Spirit and to us* to impose on you no further burden than these essentials" (Acts 15:28). The early church soon found the way in which the Holy Spirit's whisperings were best discerned: get together and talk about it. It is called the principle of synodality or conciliarity.[15] Bishops meet in council, not to find some preordained answer to a problem, but to combine their wisdom in search of an appropriate answer to a new question or problem, in the light of Jesus Christ, "the mediator and the fullness of all revelation" (*DV* 2), open to the Spirit of Reception, the Spirit of Dialogue. The hard work of ecclesial dialogue itself is the Spirit's mode of working and is indeed the Spirit's work. It is the Spirit's work if that dialogue is a simultaneous interpretation of the five Spirit-assisted criteria: scripture, tradition, *sensus fidelium,* contemporary theological scholarship, and the magisterium.

Such a pneumatology has implications for a theological anthropology, for modeling how grace and human involvement interact, for a theology of history, and for our purposes, for how the Second Vatican Council is to be received. Vatican II didn't leave us with all the answers; *it left us with a new way of being faithful to the past.* If we do want to take an insight from "exemplarism," then Vatican II is *an exemplar for the way it itself is to be interpreted.* And just as *Dei Verbum* teaches that scripture "must be read and interpreted in the sacred spirit in which it was written" (12c), so too Vatican II is to be interpreted with the same Spirit-inspired creativity that it itself exhibited.

This is the task of reception. Reception is always a *selection* from the past. From the treasure house of tradition, the church brings to the foreground what was previously neglected or explicitly rejected. Or the church might push to the background, in a new Gestalt, things that now appear less important or less helpful or even destructive. That is not to say some future generations may not want to retrieve them and bring them to the foreground once again, when *they* have to re-interpret the past from the perspective of a new time and a different context. New questions arise that the past cannot answer for us, and the past may need us to help it answer them in fidelity to the past. As O'Malley puts this new challenge:

> What this means is that we are freed from the past. We are free to appropriate what we find helpful and to reject what we find harmful. We realize, perhaps to our dismay, that we cannot simply repeat the answers of the past, for the whole situation is different. The question is different. We are different....If we are freed from the past in the sense of not expecting it to tell us what to do, we are free to make our own decisions for the future. Indeed, we have no escape from such freedom, fraught as it is with dreadful burdens.[16]

What I am calling a "reception pneumatology" would want to highlight this dreadful burden and the God-given responsibility of being active, creative, imaginative receivers of revelation—for God's sake. Vatican II was a call for a new model of traditioning and receiving the past that it itself embodied. That model requires a reception pneumatology that not only gives adequate emphasis to *both* continuity and discontinuity in the history of the tradition, but conceives the Holy Spirit as *the very source of such divine discontinuity,* for the sake of continuity with the great *traditio.*

And the divine discontinuity may just be all around us. Hence the need to be attentive to the signs of the times. John XXIII and then the Council, taking their cue from Jesus,[17] spoke of the need for discerning what God is doing in the world today, oftentimes in the disguise of nonbelievers.[18] Is this a return to an interventionist God of the "providentialism" variety, working the cards of history to some pre-set divine plan? Not necessarily. Reception pneumatology envisages the divine-human action in terms of the Holy Spirit igniting imaginative receptions of the tradition in the light of contemporary events that need to be discerned to the best of our ability.

The signs of the times can be either positive or negative. A positive sign of the times is an indicator of something new in human history, or something not before recognized as "of God," that may be revelatory of how the reign of God is erupting in the present. A negative sign of the times is an indicator of the things that are impeding the reign of God, an indicator of what is not "of God" and of what the church should be resisting.

Attention to positive and negative signs of the times is an important element in *aggiornamento.* What God's Spirit in the past, in collaboration with creative receivers, was bringing about in the world is a theological source for understanding what God's Spirit and ourselves can do now. In that sense, the past is a norm for judging the present. But just as surely, what God's Spirit is effecting in the world today with responsive human beings—and the signs of that are all around us—is a theological source for understanding, in a different way, what God was doing in the past. In that sense, the present is a norm for judging the past. Hence the theological significance of the signs of the times, that favorite theme of the Council. By the Council's own directive, the signs of the times constitute a hermeneutical lens for the very interpretation of the Council itself. Since new signs will emerge throughout history, the ongoing reception of the Council will take place from new perspectives, revealing new interpretations—in the light of the signs of the times.

And who are the troops on the ground closest to the action of God's ever-new redemptive activity in the world? The laity, as Vatican II recognized. I believe that, early in the Council's proceedings, a teaching was formulated that, in retrospect, was to become highly significant for the direction the Council would later take regarding its reform of the "how," or style, of the Catholic Church. That teaching can be found in *SC*, 14:

> Mother Church earnestly desires that all the faithful should be led to that fully conscious, and active participation in liturgical celebrations *[consciam atque actuosam liturgicarum celebrationum participationem]* which is demanded by the very nature of the liturgy. Such participation by the Christian people as "a chosen race, a royal priesthood, a holy nation, a redeemed people (1 Pet. 2:9; cf. 2:4–5), is their right and duty by reason of their baptism.
>
> In the restoration and promotion of the sacred liturgy, this full and active participation by all the people *[totius populi plena et actuosa participatio]* is the aim to be considered before all else;

for it is the primary and indispensable source from which the faithful are to derive the true Christian spirit; and therefore pastors of souls must zealously strive to achieve it, by means of the necessary instruction, in all their pastoral work. (*SC,* 14)

This fundamental shift toward "full and active participation by all the people" in the liturgy provides the hermeneutical key, I believe, not only for understanding the Council's later articulation of its ecclesial self-understanding *ad intra* in *Lumen gentium* and *ad extra* in *Gaudium et spes,* but also for stating the "spirit" of the Council as a key for interpreting the "letter" of its documents. It provides the key for later developments, such as the teachings on the People of God, the significance of the People's *sensus fidei* in ensuring faithful traditioning of revelation, the notions of *communio,* collegiality, and subsidiarity, promotion of the laity as the advance guard in the mission of the church in the world, and the need for the church to promote open dialogue with the world, with other religions, with other Christian traditions, and finally within the church itself.

As a key for interpreting the "spirit" of the Council and therefore the "letter" of its documents, one could well re-formulate into a general principle that line from *SC* 14: *The full and active participation by all the people is the aim to be considered before all else; for it is the primary and indispensable source from which the faithful are to derive the true Christian spirit.* This, I believe, sums up the "spirit" of the Council regarding the church *ad intra* and *ad extra.* Full and active participation of all the faithful means appropriate participation by the laity in the *teaching, sanctifying* and *governing* of church life, and in the mission of the church in the world, since the whole People of God, "from the Bishops down to the last of the lay faithful" (*LG,* 12, quoting Augustine) share in the prophetic, priestly, and kingly offices of Christ.[19]

By virtue of the whole people participating in Christ's prophetic office, the laity's "sense of the faith" is a crucial source and criterion for discerning the signs of the times. Of course, the *sensus laicorum* is not to be equated totally with the *sensus fidelium.* The whole body of the faithful, "from the Bishops down to the last of the lay faithful" (*LG,* 12), are the subjects of the *sensus fidei fidelium.* But, nevertheless, the *sensus laicorum* is a vital source and criterion for discerning the *sensus fidelium,* since Christ fulfils his prophetic office not only through the hierarchy but also

> through the laity whom He made His witnesses and to whom He gave understanding of the faith *[sensus fidei]* and an attractiveness in speech so that the power of the Gospel might shine forth in their daily social and family life. (*LG,* 35)

Attention to how best discern this *sensus laicorum* as a vital element in the discernment of the *sensus fidelium* in a world church is one of the urgent tasks of the Council's reception forty years on. If the Person of the Holy Spirit can be conceived as the Spirit of Reception and Dialogue between Father and Son, then it is through reception and dialogue that the workings of the Spirit are effected. Building on such a reception pneumatology, a "reception ecclesiology" is also now required that would introduce more participatory and reciprocal structures of reception and dialogue in the church.

John Paul II's call in *Novo Millennio Ineunte* for greater "structures of participation" through a "spirituality of communio"[20] will only be achieved through a spirituality of *receptio*. "To make the Church the home and school of" *receptio* would require serious implementation of the principles of dialogue and conciliarity at the local and universal level of church life to a degree hardly yet begun forty years after the Council. At the parish level, for example, priests critical of the perceived authoritarian practices of Rome are oftentimes blind to their own power politics and refusal to create opportunities for lay participation and dialogue at the local level. At the universal level, we have come to realize that not even an ecumenical council has been able to curb the power of the Roman Curia and its practices. What Cardinal Frings called for in that historic speech on November 7, 1963, has still not been satisfied: "This reform of the Curia is necessary. Let us put it into effect."[21] No micro-rupture has yet been achieved with regard to many features of the Pian era.

Forty years is still too short a period for satisfactorily assessing the results of a great conciliar event, as Alberigo suggests. But my mind keeps going back to those first days of the Council when the extraordinary happened. The documents prepared in the preparatory stage were rejected, and the Council assembly decided to start again. That decision to "start again" was a radical reform decision, a desire for micro-ruptures for the sake of continuity with the great tradition. Because of the entrenched state of the Catholicism of the Pian era, Vatican II was a new beginning like no other conciliar event. Over four years, the bishops began a renewal of what it means to be Catholic that cannot be achieved in forty years. According to their own *aggiornamento* agenda, the task is never-ending. But in forty years we have done extraordinarily well. Although some, despite their protestations to the contrary, might wish to snuff out the light on the hill that Vatican II was and is, the wind of the Spirit of the Council will not allow its own beacon to be extinguished. The gentle breeze continues to flicker the flame and make it alive. The Holy Spirit was with them; the same Holy Spirit is with us.

NOTES

Introduction

1. On the notion of "history of effect" *(Wirkungsgeschichte),* see Hans Georg Gadamer, *Truth and Method,* 2nd rev. ed. (New York: Crossroad, 1989), 300–307. On the notion of "history of reception" *(Rezeptionsgeschichte)* in the work of Hans Robert Jauss, see Ormond Rush, *The Reception of Doctrine: An Appropriation of Hans Robert Jauss' Reception Aesthetics and Literary Hermeneutics* (Rome: Gregorian University Press, 1997), 68–70.

2. Giuseppe Alberigo, "The Christian Situation after Vatican II," in *The Reception of Vatican II,* ed. Giuseppe Alberigo, Jean Pierre Jossua, and Joseph A. Komonchak (Washington, DC: Catholic University of America Press, 1987), 1–24, at 7.

3. John Henry Newman, *An Essay on the Development of Christian Doctrine,* 6th ed. (Notre Dame, IN: University of Notre Dame Press, 1989).

4. Paul Ricoeur, "The Hermeneutical Function of Distanciation," in *Hermeneutics and the Human Sciences: Essays on Language, Action and Interpretation,* ed. John B. Thompson (New York: Cambridge University Press, 1981), 131–44.

5. Quoted in Hermann J. Pottmeyer, "A New Phase in the Reception of Vatican II: Twenty Years of Interpretation of the Council," in *The Reception of Vatican II,* ed. Joseph A. Komonchak (Washington, DC: Catholic University of America Press, 1987), 27–43, at 35.

6. For a historical introduction to the hermeneutical tradition within philosophy, see Jean Grondin, *Introduction to Philosophical Hermeneutics, Yale Studies in Hermeneutics* (New Haven, CT: Yale University Press, 1994). Philosophical hermeneutics (sometimes called "general hermeneutics") seeks to articulate the dynamics of human understanding. Appropriating this philosophical reflection, more particular disciplines attempt to apply those general hermeneutical insights for their own areas of reflection (e.g., historical hermeneutics, legal hermeneutics, literary hermeneutics, theological hermeneutics). On the hermeneutical triad of understanding, interpretation, and application, see Gadamer, *Truth and Method*, 307–11.

Chapter 1

1. On "the world behind the text" and "mimesis," see Paul Ricoeur, "Time and Narrative: Threefold Mimesis," in *Time and Narrative,* vol. 1 (Chicago: University of Chicago Press, 1984), 52–87. For an appropriation of Ricoeur's framework by a biblical scholar, see Sandra Marie Schneiders, *The Revelatory Text: Interpreting the New Testament as Sacred Scripture,* 2nd ed. (Collegeville, MN: Liturgical Press, 1999), 97–179.

2. On the historical-critical method and its application to biblical interpretation, see Pontifical Biblical Commission, *The Interpretation of the Bible in the Church* (Rome: Libreria Editrice Vaticana, 1993), 34–41.

3. For a recognition that the historical context, the questions posed at the time, the linguistic forms employed, and so on, condition the original formulation of a doctrine and are significant for reconstructing the meaning of that doctrine, see Congregation for the Doctrine of the Faith, *Declaration in Defense of the Catholic Doctrine on the Church against Certain Errors of the Present Day (Mysterium Ecclesiae)* (Boston: Society of St. Paul, 1973). However,

Still Interpreting Vatican II

Peter Hünermann has remarked that just as the process of recognizing the full human character and historicity of the Bible has taken a
long time in the Catholic Church, so too it will be a long process
toward recognizing the full humanity and historicity of the church's
teachings on faith and morals. "The questions relative to a theological epistemology need to be discussed urgently in depth and to be
newly clarified on the conceptual level. The direction is clear. Just as
a long process was necessary in the church in order to arrive at the
recognition of the full human character of the Old and New
Testaments, so too an analogous process will be necessary to understand the full humanity and historicity of the teaching of the church."
Peter Hünermann, "A difesa della fede?" *Il Regno: Quindicinale di
documenti e attualità* (October 1, 1998): 565–68, at 568. For
approaches to a heremeneutics of doctrinal texts that focus mainly on
a hermeneutics of the authors and the world behind the text, see Piet
Schoonenberg, "Historicity and the Interpretation of Dogma,"
Theology Digest 18 (1970): 132–43; Walter Principe, "The
Hermeneutic of Roman Catholic Dogmatic Statements," *Studies in
Religion/Sciences Religieuses* 2 (1972): 157–75; Avery Dulles, "The
Hermeneutics of Dogmatic Statements," in *The Survival of Dogma:
Faith, Authority, and Dogma in a Changing World* (New York:
Crossroad Press, 1987), 171–84.

    4. Giuseppe Alberigo and Joseph A. Komonchak, eds.,
*History of Vatican II, Vol. 1: Announcing and Preparing Vatican
Council II* (Maryknoll, NY: Orbis Books, 1996); Giuseppe
Alberigo and Joseph A. Komonchak, eds., *History of Vatican II,
Vol. 2: The Formation of the Council's Identity, First Period and
Intersession, October 1962–September 1963* (Maryknoll, NY: Orbis
Books, 1997); Giuseppe Alberigo and Joseph A. Komonchak, eds.,
*History of Vatican II, Vol. 3: The Mature Council: Second Period
and Intersession, September 1963–September 1964* (Maryknoll, NY:
Orbis Books, 1996); Giuseppe Alberigo and Joseph A.
Komonchak, *History of Vatican II, Vol. 4: Church as Communion,*

Notes

Third Period and Intersession, September 1964–September 1965 (Maryknoll, NY: Orbis Books, 2003).

5. For commentary on the drafting of all documents, see the five volumes of the classic work edited by Herbert Vorgrimler, *Commentary on the Documents of Vatican II* (London: Burns & Oates, 1967). Other representative works can be cited. On *Lumen gentium* in particular, see Gérard Philips, *L'Église et son mystère au II Concile du Vatican: Histoire, texte et commentaire de la Constitution Lumen Gentium* (Paris: Desclée, 1967). On *Dei Verbum,* see Luis Alonso Schökel and Antonio María Artola, *La Palabra de Dios en la historia de los hombres: comentario temático a la Constitución "Dei Verbum" del Vaticano II sobre la divina revelación* (Bilbao: Universidad de Deusto: Ediciones Mensajero, 1991); Hanjo Sauer, *Erfahrung und Glaube: die Begründung des pastoralen Prinzips durch die Offenbarungskonstitution des II. Vatikanischen Konzils, Würzburger Studien zur Fundamentaltheologie, Bd. 12* (Frankfurt am Main/New York: P. Lang, 1993). On the drafting of *Dignitatis humanae* on religious freedom, see Richard J. Regan, *Conflict and Consensus: Religious Freedom and the Second Vatican Council* (New York: Macmillan, 1967).

6. For a more precise use of the term, see Joseph A. Komonchak, "Vatican II as an 'Event,'" *Theology Digest* 46 (1999): 337–52, which is the text of a talk summarizing and developing his earlier "Riflessioni storiografiche sul Vaticano II come evento," in *L'Evento e le decisioni: Studi sulle dinamiche del Concilio vaticano II,* ed. Maria Teresa Fattori and Alberto Melloni (Bologna: Il mulino, 1997), 417–49. I will be returning to Komonchak's usage of "event" as a category for historical occurrences that, when judged retrospectively, are evaluated as constituting an epochal change or rupture. For the purposes of my framework, Komonchak's more precise sense of the term will have relevance in discussion of the history of the Council's reception over the last forty years.

7. For example, on the individual believer's reception of revelation, see Ormond Rush, "*Sensus Fidei:* Faith Making Sense of Revelation," *Theological Studies* 62 (2001): 231–61. For a survey of the use of the category in contemporary theology, see Gilles Routhier, "Reception in Current Theological Debate," in *Reception and Communion Among Churches,* ed. Hervé Legrand, Julio Manzanares, and Antonio García y García (Washington, DC: Catholic University of America Press, 1997), 17–52, at 41–44.

8. While not wanting to equate the history of salvation completely with church history, a similar point is being made by claiming that "no separation is possible between 'the history of salvation' and 'the history of the world.'" See Giuseppe Ruggieri, "Faith and History," in *The Reception of Vatican II,* ed. Giuseppe Alberigo, Jean Pierre Jossua, and Joseph A. Komonchak (Washington, DC: The Catholic University of America Press, 1987), 91–114, at 104.

9. Applying a teaching of the Council itself as a principle for its own interpretation, we could highlight the notion of "living tradition" captured in *DV,* 8a: "What was handed on by the apostles comprises everything that serves to make the people of God live their lives in holiness and increase their faith. In this way the church, in its doctrine, life and worship, perpetuates and transmits to every generation all that it itself is, all that it believes." The French Dominican *peritus* Yves Congar was highly influential in the drafting of this text. For his seminal work on the notion of "living tradition," see Yves Congar, *Tradition and Traditions: An Historical and a Theological Essay* (New York: The Macmillan Company, 1966) and Congar's synthesis of that work in Yves Congar, *The Meaning of Tradition* (New York: Hawthorn Books, 1964).

10. The first term *ressourcement* emerged as a common phrase to describe the work of historical theologians in the decades leading up to the Council. The phrase was originally used in a derogatory sense by Reginald Garrigou-Lagrange in reference to the theology of Henri de Lubac and others. The neologism *aggiornamento* was not

created by Pope John XXIII, although he made it his own. Gathering in Rome in 1950, the first International Congress of Religious was meeting, according to Cardinal Piazza, for the purpose of "*aggiornamento* of the orders and congregations." Quoted in Étienne Fouilloux, "The Antepreparatory Phase: The Slow Emergence from Inertia (January 1959–October 1962)," in *History of Vatican II, Vol. 1: Announcing and Preparing Vatican Council II,* ed. Giuseppe Alberigo and Joseph A. Komonchak (Maryknoll, NY: Orbis Books, 1996), 55–166, at 72n22.

11. For examples of the Council's desire to be in continuity with the past tradition, see *AAS* 57 (1965): 12, 24–25, 27, 39, 44, 55, 58; 58 (1966): 702, 706, 845, 952. This tradition is also seen extending to the time of Israel and into the eschatological future: see *AAS* 54 (1962): 8; 57 (1965): 5, 22, 57; 58 (1966): 727, 817.

12. Walter Kasper, "The Continuing Challenge of the Second Vatican Council: The Hermeneutics of the Conciliar Statements," in *Theology and Church* (New York: Crossroad, 1989), 166–76, at 172.

13. Synod of Bishops, "Final Report," in *Documents of the Extraordinary Synod of Bishops November 28–December 8, 1985* (Homebush, Australia: St. Paul Publications, 1986), 22.

14. Joseph Ratzinger and Vittorio Messori, *The Ratzinger Report: An Exclusive Interview on the State of the Church* (San Francisco: Ignatius Press, 1985), 35. For further information on Ratzinger's approach to retrieving "the true Council," see Joseph Cardinal Ratzinger, *Principles of Catholic Theology: Building Stones for a Fundamental Theology* (San Francisco: Ignatius Press, 1987), 367–93. For an earlier "pre-1968" interpretation of the Council, see Joseph Ratzinger, "Catholicism After the Council," *The Furrow* 18 (1967): 3–23.

15. As we will see, I believe Ratzinger is simplifying the complex dynamics between tradition and reception, tradition and innovation, continuity and discontinuity.

16. Otto Hermann Pesch, *Das Zweite Vaticanische Konzil: Vorgeschichte–Verlauf–Ergebnisse–Nachgeschichte* (Würzburg: Echter Verlag, 2001), 149.

17. In reference to the contemporary church's task of rethinking the faith, just as the early church had to rethink its Jewish faith on the basis of what they had experienced in Jesus Christ, Giuseppe Ruggieri writes: "Here we find ourselves facing a new beginning. In an unprecedented form, a pluralism of culture and peoples is emerging which, in the historical awareness that we now have of this pluralism and its dignity, is not comparable with that of past eras. But the 'beginning' is not an absolute beginning. That would be unthinkable for Christians. No one can build on a foundation other than the 'which has been laid.' Rather, it is a matter of a creative interpretation which rediscovers possibilities in the tradition of which it has never previously made use, because past history did not draw on them or even thought that they were ruled out." Giuseppe Ruggieri, "Towards a Hermeneutic of Vatican II," *Concilium* 1 (1999): 1–13, at 5–6.

18. John W. O'Malley, "Vatican II: Official Norms. On Interpreting the Council, with a Response to Cardinal Avery Dulles," *America*, 31 March 2003, 12.

19. Pesch goes on to state (Pesch, *Das Zweite Vaticanische Konzil*, 149–50) that even "innovations" are to be presumed as serving continuity with this greater tradition: "New ideas in the Council texts are to be viewed, until proving the opposite, not as 'innovations' but rather as a critical opening of narrow directions of the last hundred years by means of an invigorating of the old tradition. Such invigoration is legitimate since it represents, not a special tradition of the Western church, but rather represents the tradition of the universal church." He goes on to apply this to Vatican I and its innovation regarding papal infallibility. O'Malley, likewise, states: "As a principle of historical method, the continuities in history must, I believe, always and invariably be given the benefit of the doubt as being stronger than the discontinuities, even when we deal with what

Thomas Kuhn taught us to call paradigm shifts." See O'Malley, "Vatican II: Official Norms. On Interpreting the Council, with a Response to Cardinal Avery Dulles," 12.

20. See John W. O'Malley, "Reform, Historical Consciousness, and Vatican II's *Aggiornamento*," in *Tradition and Transition: Historical Perspectives on Vatican II* (Wilmington, DE: M. Glazier, 1989), 44–81.

21. "Immediately after the council participants hailed it as 'the end of the Counter-Reformation,' 'the end of the Constantinian era,' even as a 'new Pentecost.' Well, we all get carried away sometimes. Today these expressions may seem overwrought, even though in my opinion the first two capture essential features of the changes the Council effected. In any case, all three indicate that at the time, participants in the Council were convinced that something of deep significance had happened. This conviction was not restricted to a small handful of bishops but was by far the dominant view." John W. O'Malley, "The Style of Vatican II: The 'How' of the Church Changed during the Council," *America*, February 24, 2003, 12–15.

22. For a full discussion on this awareness at Vatican II, see Ruggieri, "Faith and History."

23. Ruggieri, "Towards a Hermeneutic of Vatican II," 3.

24. Kasper, "The Continuing Challenge," 171.

25. The Council was here receiving the work of the Pontifical Biblical Commission's 1964 document on the historical nature of the Gospels. Were a council to be called today, it would no doubt receive the commission's later document on methods beyond the historical-critical approach.

26. Pope Leo XIII, *The Restoration of Christian Philosophy (Aeterni Patris)* (Boston: St. Paul Books and Media, no date).

27. On the thesis that "the Blondelian perspective exerted a powerful influence at Vatican Council II," see Gregory Baum, *Man Becoming: God in Secular Language* (New York: Herder and Herder, 1970), 1–36, at 29. On Henri de Lubac, see Joseph A. Komonchak,

"Theology and Culture at Mid-Century: The Example of Henri de Lubac," *Theological Studies* 51 (1990): 579–602; Joseph A. Komonchak, "Recapturing the Great Tradition. In Memoriam: Henri de Lubac," *Commonweal* 119 (January 31, 1992): 14–17. On Maritain, Chenu, and de Lubac, see Joseph A. Komonchak, "Returning from Exile: Catholic Theology in the 1930s," in *The Twentieth Century: A Theological Overview,* ed. Gregory Baum (Maryknoll, NY: Orbis Books, 1999), 35–48. For an excellent survey of Catholic theology from the Modernist crisis to Vatican II, see also the chapters by Francis Schüssler Fiorenza in James C. Livingston et al., *Modern Christian Thought. Volume 2: The Twentieth Century,* 2nd ed. (Upper Saddle River, NJ: Prentice Hall, 2000), 197–271. See also Mark Schoof, *A Survey of Catholic Theology* 1800–1970 (New York: Paulist Press, 1970).

28. On Catholic theology from the Modernist crisis to Vatican II, see Dan Donovan, "Modernism and Vatican II," *Grail: An Ecumenical Journal* 2 (1986): 57–68.

29. Ladislas Örsy, in *The Church Learning and Teaching* (Dublin: Dominican Publications, 1987), 97n15, writes: "The success of Vatican Council II was due as much to the insights of the theologians as to the judgments of the bishops. It was an ideally construed situation for progress. To begin with, the theologians were trusted; they were officially invited to contribute. They came not only from all places, but from all schools of thought. They did much of the work by themselves; then they put their insights before commissions composed of theologians and bishops who did much of the screening, selecting and deciding what should be put before the plenary assembly. Finally, the bishops voted at their general congregations. Throughout it all there was a balanced play. The daring insights (or the pedestrian thinking) of the theologians were subject to the 'Christian common sense' approach of the bishops; that is, intellectual discourses were measured by pastoral effectiveness. The final documents are the results of such a play, which was both creative and moderating." See also Karl Heinz

Neufeld, "In the Service of the Council: Bishops and Theologians at the Second Vatican Council (for Cardinal Henri de Lubac on His Ninetieth Birthday)," in *Vatican II: Assessment and Perspectives. Twenty-Five Years After,* vol. 1 *(1962–1987),* ed. René Latourelle (New York: Paulist Press, 1988), 74–105; Herbert Vorgrimler, "Karl Rahner: The Theologian's Contribution," in *Vatican II by Those Who Were There,* ed. Alberic Stacpoole (London: Geoffrey Chapman, 1986), 32–46; J. F. Kobler, "Were Theologians the Engineers of Vatican II?" *Gregorianum* 70 (1989): 233–50.

30. For example, see the study by Charles Henry Miller, *"As It Is Written": The Use of Old Testament References in the Documents of Vatican Council II* (St. Louis, MO: Marianist Communications Center, 1973).

31. Many examples could be given of the impact of biblical scholarship on the direction of the conciliar teachings. For example, the biblical notion of "the people of God" is highly significant in the discussion regarding the structure and direction of *Lumen gentium.* See Yves Congar, "The People of God," in *Vatican II: An Interfaith Appraisal,* ed. John H. Miller (Notre Dame, IN: University of Notre Dame Press, 1966), 197–207.

32. For example, on the quotation of patristic sources in *Lumen gentium,* see Henri de Lubac, *"Lumen Gentium* and the Fathers," in *Vatican II: An Interfaith Appraisal,* ed. John H. Miller (Notre Dame, IN: University of Notre Dame Press, 1966), 153–75.

33. See also *AAS* 54 (1962): 8; 57 (1965): 5, 22, 57; 58 (1966): 727, 817.

34. Pottmeyer, "A New Phase in the Reception of Vatican II," 33.

35. For a comprehensive survey of theologians and directions in Scholasticism from its early beginnings in the sixth century to its post-Thomas developments till the eighteenth century, see Ulrich G. Leinsle, *Einführung in die scholastische Theologie* (Paderborn: Ferdinand Schöningh, 1995). On the nineteenth century, see Gerald

A. McCool, *Nineteenth-Century Scholasticism: The Search for a Unitary Method* (New York: Fordham University Press, 1989).

36. On the breakdown of a monolithic interpretation of Thomism in the twentieth century due to historical-critical studies by historians of theology and the consequently diverse and divergent interpretations, see Gerald A. McCool, *From Unity to Pluralism: The Internal Evolution of Thomism* (New York: Fordham University Press, 1989); Francis Schüssler Fiorenza, "The New Theology and Transcendental Thomism," in *Modern Christian Thought. Volume 2: The Twentieth Century,* ed. James C. Livingston, et al. (Upper Saddle River, NJ: Prentice Hall, 2000), 197–232; Thomas F. O'Meara, *Thomas Aquinas Theologian* (Notre Dame, IN: University of Notre Dame Press, 1997), 152–200; Fergus Kerr, *After Aquinas: Versions of Thomism* (Oxford: Blackwell Publishing, 2002); Joseph A. Komonchak, "Thomism and the Second Vatican Council," in *Continuity and Plurality in Catholic Theology: Essays in Honor of Gerald A. McCool,* ed. Anthony J. Cernera (Fairfield, CT: Sacred Heart University Press, 1998), 53–73.

37. See Komonchak, "Thomism and the Second Vatican Council," 62: "The twentieth century would see a variety of 'Thomisms': those of Gardeil, Maritain, Gilson, Rousselot and Maréchal, Rahner and Lonergan, Mercier and the Louvain school, Garrigou-Lagrange, and Chenu, not to mention the Suarezian Thomism that reigned among Jesuits in the early decades of the century, what de Lubac calls 'the mongrel Thomism' of *Action Française,* and the 'paleo-Thomism' that Van Steenberghen says reigned in Rome among 'Thomists of the strict observance.'"

38. In reference to the bishops' rejection of the draft on revelation presented to them, Joseph Ratzinger, in his 1966 commentary on the Council, comments: "The rejection of the proposed draft as inadequate also implied a demand for a fresh start. The reversal had profound and exciting implications. What was at stake was not this or that theory, this or that special scholarly question, but the form in

which the Word of God was to be presented and spiritually interpreted. Here the preparatory effort was unsatisfactory, and the Council rejected the extant texts. But the question at this point was: What now?" Joseph Ratzinger, *Theological Highlights of Vatican II* (New York: Paulist Press, 1966), 148. This question would arise throughout discussion of all topics where the bishops reject the schemas of the preparatory commission because of the predominance of their Scholastic framework.

39. This phrase recurs throughout the writings of Ratzinger on Vatican II. He not only uses it to describe the attitude of the Council but also that of Pope John XXIII.

40. Of course, this typology is somewhat simplistic, since many of those wanting to retain the achievements of Aquinas also were wanting to retrieve the fruits of the great patristic enterprise and the ecclesiology of the first millennium, e.g., Congar.

41. Despite his own attempt to retrieve "the real Thomas" from his later misinterpreters, de Lubac remained suspicious of the Thomistic project. See Joseph A. Komonchak, "Vatican II and the Encounter between Catholicism and Liberalism," in *Catholicism and Liberalism: Contributions to American Public Philosophy,* ed. R. Bruce Douglass and David Hollenbach (Cambridge: Cambridge University Press, 1994), 76–99, at 98n20: "Although de Lubac's *Surnaturel* was in good part an effort to rescue Thomas from the Thomists, it is also clear that de Lubac believed that many traces of original sin remained after Aquinas's effort to 'baptize' Aristotle."

42. For examples, see Giacomo Martina, "The Historical Context in Which the Idea of a New Ecumenical Council Was Born," in *Vatican II: Assessment and Perspectives: Twenty-Five Years After (1962–1987),* ed. René Latourelle (New York: Paulist Press, 1988), 3–73.

43. See Joseph A. Komonchak, "Modernity and the Construction of Roman Catholicism," *Cristianesimo nella storia* 18 (1997): 353–85.

44. Komonchak, "Vatican II and the Encounter between Catholicism and Liberalism," at 76.

45. Still helpful for understanding the diverse approaches taken to this issue during and after the Council is the typology outlined in H. Richard Niebuhr, *Christ and Culture*, 1st ed. (New York: Harper, 1951).

46. Kenneth Clark, *Civilisation: A Personal View* (London: British Broadcasting Corporation, 1969), 17.

47. George H. Tavard, "Reassessing the Reformation," *One in Christ* 19 (1983): 354–67.

48. Ormond Rush, "The Offices of Christ, *Lumen Gentium* and the People's Sense of the Faith," *Pacifica* 16 (2003): 137–52.

49. Quoted in Pottmeyer, "A New Phase in the Reception of Vatican II," 35.

50. Pesch, *Das Zweite Vaticanische Konzil,* 160.

51. Kasper, "The Continuing Challenge of the Second Vatican Council," 172.

52. John O'Malley writes of the significance of "slogans" in the Gregorian reform and the Lutheran Reformation, and of the similar use of "slogans" in the discourse of Vatican II. See John W. O'Malley, "Developments, Reforms, and Two Great Reformations: Towards a Historical Assessment of Vatican II," in *Tradition and Transition: Historical Perspectives on Vatican II* (Wilmington, DE: M. Glazier, 1989), 82–125 at 98–99; 111–15.

53. See Karl Rahner, "Basic Theological Interpretation of the Second Vatican Council," in *Theological Investigations* (London: Darton, Longman & Todd, 1981), 77–89; Karl Rahner, "The Abiding Significance of the Second Vatican Council," in *Theological Investigations,* volume 20 (London: Darton, Longman & Todd, 1981), 90–102.

54. Kasper, "The Continuing Challenge of the Second Vatican Council," 172.

55. Alberigo, "The Christian Situation after Vatican II," 16.

56. John W. O'Malley, "Vatican II: Historical Perspectives on Its Uniqueness and Interpretation," in *Vatican II, The Unfinished Agenda: A Look to the Future,* ed. Lucien Richard, Daniel J. Harrington, and John W. O'Malley (New York: Paulist Press, 1987), 22–32 at 26–27: "What in fact did happen emerges only when we place the documents in their precise historical context and do not treat them as enunciations of eternally valid platitudes. If we follow such a methodology, a fair, but not exhaustive, list of the aims of the Council would go something like this: [1] to end the stance of cultural isolation that the Church was now seen as having maintained; [2] to initiate a new freedom of expression and action within the Church that certain Vatican institutions were now interpreted as having previously curtailed; [3] to distribute more broadly the exercise of pastoral authority, especially by strengthening the role of episcopacy and local church vis-à-vis the Holy See; [4] to modify in people's consciousness and in the actual functioning of the Church the predominantly clerical, institutional and hierarchical model that had prevailed; [5] to affirm the dignity of the laity in the Church; [6] to establish through a more conciliatory attitude, through some new theological insights, and through effective mechanisms a better relationship with other religious bodies, looking ultimately to the healing of the divisions in Christianity and the fruitful 'dialogue' with non-Christian religions; [7] to change the teaching of the Church on 'religious liberty' and to give new support to the principle of 'freedom of conscience'; [8] to base theology and biblical studies more firmly on historical principles; [9] to foster [new styles of piety]; [10] to affirm clearly that the Church was and should be affected by the cultures in which its exists; [11] finally, to promote a more positive appreciation of 'the world' and the relationship of the Church to it, with a concomitant assumption of clearer responsibility for the fate of the world in 'the new era' that the Council saw opening up before its eyes. Surprisingly enough for some of us, the present conflict over interpretation of the Council revolves around just how seriously and radically these goals are to be taken—

and in certain instances, it seems, whether they were really goals at all." (The list was numbered by the author for easier reading.)

57. Ratzinger and Messori, *The Ratzinger Report,* 31.

58. Ibid., 34.

59. I take the phrase from John O'Malley, who is speaking generally of those who do not interpret the Council as an event with radical implications. See O'Malley, "Vatican II: Historical Perspectives," 24.

60. This second sense of "the Spirit of the Council" requires that we explicitly bring into consideration a *theological hermeneutics* informed by a particular *pneumatology.* That pneumatology will need to be coherent with a *theological anthropology,* a theology of the way *grace* works in human affairs, and a *theology of history* that envisages God's involvement in human affairs according to a particular model. The importance of active human reception of revelation should guide each of these theologies. Furthermore, each of these theologies should be consistently applied when we come to speak of the contemporary reception of the Council forty years later. The same Holy Spirit, working according to the same principles, is at work guiding faithful reception of the Council. Appropriating *DV,* 12c, the Council should be interpreted "in the sacred spirit in which it was written." This will be addressed in greater detail in the section on the reception of the Council.

61. O'Malley, "Reform, Historical Consciousness, and Vatican II's *Aggiornamento,*" 45.

62. Pottmeyer, "A New Phase in the Reception of Vatican II," 37.

63. For a history of the leitmotif and the particular literary battle, see Hans Robert Jauss, "Antiqui/moderni (Querelle des Anciens et des Modernes)," in *Historisches Wörterbuch der Philosophie,* ed. Joachim Ritter (Basel/Stuttgart: Schwabe & Co., 1971), 410–14; Hans Robert Jauss, "Ursprung und Bedeutung der Fortschrittsidee in der 'Querelle des Anciens et des Modernes,'" in *Die Philosophie*

und die Frage nach dem Fortschritt, ed. H. Kuhn and R. Wiedmann (Munich: Pustet, 1964).

64. "The will to compromise is simply the will to remain united as long as the truth of the faith itself is not at issue, and to preserve *communio* with one another and continuity in doctrine." Pottmeyer, "A New Phase in the Reception of Vatican II," 38.

65. Pesch, *Das Zweite Vaticanische Konzil,* 150.

66. Ibid., 150.

67. See Ibid., 150–54.

68. Quoted in John F. Long, "From One Who Was There," *America,* March 17, 2003, 14.

69. Pottmeyer, "A New Phase in the Reception of Vatican II," 38. Kasper likewise points out that it is the ecclesial task of theologians to find more coherent and systematic ways of maintaining the tensions that the Council left unresolved: "Admittedly, the harmonization between earlier and later tradition is often not completely successful; for—like most previous councils—Vatican II solved its task, not with the help of a comprehensive theory, but by pegging out the limits of the church's position. In this sense it was completely in the conciliar tradition for a juxtaposition to remain. As in the case of every council, the theoretical mediation of these positions is *a task for the theology that comes afterwards.*" Kasper, "The Continuing Challenge of the Second Vatican Council," 171 (my italics).

70. Pesch, *Das Zweite Vaticanische Konzil,* 157.

71. Pottmeyer, "A New Phase in the Reception of Vatican II," 39.

72. See Komonchak, "Vatican II and the Encounter between Catholicism and Liberalism," 96n9: "Pope John did not counterpose the 'doctrinal' to the 'pastoral,' as if the latter were simply a matter of 'applications,' but saw the pastoral dimension as a 'historical imperative' intrinsic to doctrine: 'the historical hermeneutics of Christian truth.'" Komonchak is quoting Giuseppe Ruggieri, "Appunti per una

teologia in Papa Roncalli," in *Papa Giovanni,* ed. Giuseppe Alberigo (Bari: Laterza, 1987), 245–71, at 256.

73. Ruggieri, "Towards a Hermeneutic of Vatican II," 7 (my italics).

74. In the next section we will revisit this rhetorical aspect of the documents.

75. See Rush, "The Offices of Christ," 146n43.

76. *GS,* 4; *PO,* 9; *AA,* 14; *UR,* 4. On John XXIII's deliberate focus on positive signs of the times, as a rejection of the prevailing negativity in the church regarding the surrounding culture and society, see Ruggieri, "Towards a Hermeneutic of Vatican II," 6–8. It is this deliberate focus on the positive that Ratzinger has called John XXIII's "naïve optimism."

77. Synod of Bishops, "Final Report," 22.

78. "Canonical reception" refers to the assent (or otherwise) given by the believer to a particular teaching in response to the call to obedience by the teaching authority. That response may vary from simple acceptance to outright rejection or dissent. "Hermeneutical reception," on the other hand, refers to the believer's attempt to understand, interpret, and apply that teaching in their life context. In the case of canonical dissent, it may mean that a believer has been unable to understand, interpret, and apply a teaching to their own life.

79. See Francis A. Sullivan, "Evaluation and Interpretation of the Documents of Vatican II," in *Creative Fidelity: Weighing and Interpreting Documents of the Magisterium* (New York: Paulist Press, 1996), 162–74.

80. Regarding the insufficiency of the historical-critical method by itself for the interpretation of the *biblical* texts, see Pontifical Biblical Commission, *The Interpretation of the Bible in the Church,* 41: "No scientific method for the study of the Bible is fully adequate to comprehend the biblical texts in all their richness. For all its overall validity, the historical-critical method cannot claim to be totally sufficient in this respect. It necessarily has to leave aside many

aspects of the writings which it studies. It is not surprising, then, that at the present time, other methods and approaches are proposed which serve to explore more profoundly other aspects worthy of attention."

Chapter 2

1. "The traditional style of conciliar documents has been the terse form of the canon, which in a few words proscribed some belief or practice. The canons reflect by their form the presumption that a council is basically a judicial or legislative body, convoked to resolve some immediate and well-defined problem or set of problems. The language is, within certain limits, juridical and precise. The first real break in this tradition came with the Council of Trent, which decided to issue along with canons the so-called 'chapters' that would present the positive teaching against which the ideas condemned in the canons erred." See O'Malley, "Vatican II: Historical Perspectives," 25–26.

2. See, for example, Principe, "The Hermeneutic of Roman Catholic Dogmatic Statements"; Dulles, "The Hermeneutics of Dogmatic Statements."

3. Rahner, "Basic Theological Interpretation," 89, states: "At least in *Gaudium et Spes* the Council adopted spontaneously a mode of expression which had the character neither of dogmatic teaching valid for all time nor of canonical enactments, but was perhaps to be understood as the expression of 'instructions' or 'appeals' (presupposing a theory about official ecclesiastical statements which is not yet by any means explicit, since in this respect we are familiar only with dogmatic statements and official enactments and orders)."

4 See Pontifical Biblical Commission, *The Interpretation of the Bible in the Church*, 41–44. See also Alan G. Gross and William M.

Keith, *Rhetorical Hermeneutics: Invention and Interpretation in the Age of Science* (Albany: State University of New York Press, 1997).

5. Gerard Hall, "Catholic Church Teaching on its Relationship to Other Religions since Vatican II" (paper presented at the Australian Catholic Theological Association, Melbourne, July 2002).

6. See John W. O'Malley, "Erasmus and Vatican II: Interpreting the Council," in *Cristianesimo nella storia: saggi in onore di Giuseppe Alberigo,* ed. Alberto Melloni, et al. (Bologna: Il Mulino, 1996), 195–211, at 211: "I believe an examination of Erasmus can provide hermeneutical clues for understanding and interpreting the council, in great part because it places the council on a much broader historical canvas than most attempts to interpret it do. It fits the council in the rhetorical/literary tradition, and for once at least gets us out of theologians' obsessive focus on the philosophical tradition. It forces us to take style and literary form into account to a degree most interpretations do not. Here, if ever, style and content cannot be separated. Here, if ever, the style is the council." For further background on the echoes of *"ars laudandi"* in Vatican II, see John W. O'Malley, *Praise and Blame in Renaissance Rome: Rhetoric, Doctrine, and Reform in the Sacred Orators of the Papal Court, c. 1450–1521* (Durham, NC: Duke University Press, 1979), 36–76. See also John W. O'Malley, "Culture Three," in *The Four Cultures of Europe* (forthcoming).

7. O'Malley, "Vatican II: Historical Perspectives," 25. Elsewhere O'Malley writes: "The 'rhetoric of reproach' is replaced by a 'rhetoric of congratulation.' This stance may well be religiously admirable, but it is rhetorically problematic; for it induces a vagueness and indeterminacy into language that deprives it of dramatic force." See O'Malley, "Developments, Reforms, and Two Great Reformations," 112.

8. Elsewhere he formulates this insight into a hermeneutical norm: "In order to understand the relationship between the spirit and

the letter of the council, due attention must be given to the style and literary forms in which the teaching of the council finds expression." John W. O'Malley, "Vatican II: Official Norms. On Interpreting the Council, with a Response to Cardinal Avery Dulles," *America*, March 31, 2003, 11–14, at 12.

9. O'Malley, "Erasmus and Vatican II," 197.

10. Ratzinger and Messori, *The Ratzinger Report*, 31. "The reading of the *letter* of the documents will enable us to discover their true *spirit*. If thus discovered in their truth, those great texts will make it possible for us to understand just what happened and to react with a new vigor." Ratzinger and Messori, *The Ratzinger Report*, 40.

11. John W. O'Malley, "Vatican II: A Matter of Style," in *Weston Jesuit School of Theology 2003 President's Letter* (Cambridge, MA: Weston Jesuit School of Theology, 2003), 3.

12. Ibid., 5.

13. Ibid. The style of being church that Vatican II rejected was the peculiarly modern style the church took on in reaction to the Enlightenment and the French Revolution: "As the evils of democracy spread, the papacy began to function in ever more autocratic fashion, even in dealing with bishops. Under Pius X in the early twentieth century the Holy Office of the Inquisition began to function with a vigor it had not known since it was instituted in the sixteenth century, issuing excommunications and forbidding discussion of crucial issues. A new papacy and a new papal style had come into being that emphasized, almost to the point of caricature, the authoritarian strains in the Catholic tradition and that set the church against and above almost every person and idea outside it. True, Benedict XV, Pius XI, and Pius XII tempered these ideas and policies, yet the basic elements of the style prevailed....It was a change in this closed, ghetto like, condemnatory, authoritarian style that the Council wanted to effect." O'Malley, "Vatican II: A Matter of Style," 6.

14. On the changing structure of the various drafts, see Giuseppe Alberigo and Franca Magistretti, "Appendix B: Conspectus

Schematum," in *Constitutionis Dogmaticae Lumen Gentium: Synopsis Historica* (Bologna: Istituto per le Scienze Religiose, 1975), xxvii–xxxvii.

15. See Rush, "The Offices of Christ," 150.

16. Ignace de la Potterie, "Interpretation of Holy Scripture in the Spirit in Which It Was Written (*Dei Verbum*, 12c)," in *Vatican II: Assessment and Perspectives. Twenty-Five Years After (1962–1987)*, ed. René Latourelle (New York: Paulist Press, 1988), 220–66, at 235.

17. Synod of Bishops, "Final Report," 22.

18. See *DV*, 18.

19. Synod of Bishops, "Final Report," 22.

20. On the distinction between "weighing" and "interpreting," see Sullivan, "Evaluation and Interpretation of the Documents of Vatican II."

21. Rahner, "Basic Theological Interpretation," 81.

22. Ibid., 81–82.

23. Ibid., 82.

24. Pottmeyer, "A New Phase in the Reception of Vatican II," 32.

25. O'Malley, "Vatican II: Historical Perspectives," 24.

26. Ratzinger, *Principles of Catholic Theology*, 378–79.

27. "This tradition which comes from the Apostles develops in the Church with the help of the Holy Spirit. For there is a growth in the understanding of the realities and the words which have been handed down....For as the centuries succeed one another, the Church constantly moves forward toward the fullness of divine truth until the words of God reach their complete fulfillment in her" (*DV*, 8). The "growth in understanding" that took place in the space of four years is an important factor in interpreting the whole Council faithfully.

28. Synod of Bishops, "Final Report," 22 (my italics).

29. See Graham Allen, *Intertextuality* (New York: Routledge, 2000).

30. Ibid., 1.

31. Umberto Eco, *The Name of the Rose* (London: Vintage, 1998), 286. Quoted in Allen, *Intertextuality*, 198.

32. Synod of Bishops, "Final Report," 22.

33. O'Malley, "Vatican II: Historical Perspectives," 26.

34. Pottmeyer, "A New Phase in the Reception of Vatican II," 42.

35. O'Malley, "Vatican II: Historical Perspectives," 23.

36. "Whether Vatican II was in any sense responsible for the dramatic changes in Catholicism cannot be settled simply by ascertaining the intentions of participants or by examining the final texts. Social scientists speak of a law of unintended consequences: no historical agent can know in advance all the consequences of an action. Historians are not content to uncover what people in the past intended or desired to do; they also look for links and sequences among events that were unknown to contemporaries but which later and fuller perspectives can identify." Joseph A. Komonchak, "40 Years after Vatican II: The Ongoing Challenge," *Ligourian*, October 2002, 11–14, at 14.

Chapter 3

1. Ratzinger rightly recalls that "not every valid council in the history of the Church has been a fruitful one; in the last analysis, many of them have been just a waste of time [he cites the ineffectiveness of the Fifth Lateran Council, 1512–1517, in averting the crisis of the Reformation]. Despite all the good to be found in the texts it produced, the last word about the historical value of Vatican Council II has yet to be spoken. If, in the end, it will be numbered among the highlights of Church history depends on those who will transform its words into the life of the Church." Ratzinger, *Principles of Catholic Theology*, 378.

2. Kasper, "The Continuing Challenge of the Second Vatican Council," 168.

3. Ratzinger, *Principles of Catholic Theology*, 374–75. Ratzinger further highlights the importance of a Council's reception, or assimilation, into the life of the church (377): "Whether or not the Council becomes a positive force in the history of the Church depends only indirectly on texts and organizations; the crucial question is whether there are individuals—saints—who, by their personal willingness, which cannot be forced, are ready to effect something new and living. The ultimate decision about the historical significance of Vatican Council II depends on whether or not there are individuals prepared to experience in themselves the drama of the separation of the wheat from the cockle and thus to give to the whole a singleness of meaning that it cannot gain from words alone."

4. Alberigo, "The Christian Situation after Vatican II," 24. Likewise Pottmeyer asserts: "From the standpoint of an ecclesiology of communion, the entire people of God is the subject that receives. If reception is not a merely passive process, then the entire people of God, though in varying ways, plays an active role in interpreting a council." Pottmeyer, "A New Phase in the Reception of Vatican II," 30. It is important also to note that, as *Lumen gentium* teaches, the People of God is not to be equated with the laity alone. The People of God includes all, "from the bishops to the last of the faithful," as *LG,* 12 puts it, quoting Augustine. The *sensus fidei fidelium* is not to be simplistically and exclusively identified with some *sensus laicorum,* although the former certainly includes the latter.

5. Rahner, "Basic Theological Interpretation"; Rahner, "The Abiding Significance of the Second Vatican Council."

6. J. M. R. Tillard, "Reception—Communion," *One in Christ* 28 (1992): 307–22, at 307. Tillard is writing of the twentieth century.

7. For example, see the collection of articles in World Council of Churches, *Councils and the Ecumenical Movement,* vol. 5 (Geneva: WCC, 1968).

8. Alois Grillmeier, "Konzil und Rezeption. Methodische Bemerkungen zu einem Thema der ökumenischen Diskussion der Gegenwart," *Theologie und Philosophie* 45 (1970): 321–52; Yves Congar, "La 'Réception' comme réalité ecclésiologique," *Revue des Sciences Philosophiques et Théologiques* 56 (1972): 369–402.

9. For a summary of Grillmeier's and Congar's writings on the reception of councils in the early church, see Rush, *The Reception of Doctrine,* 125–61. Grillmeier and Congar did not so much focus on councils themselves as events of reception, as I have done in the first section above. Their concern is the life of a council after it had closed.

10. See Alois Grillmeier, *Christ in Christian Tradition. Volume Two: From the Council of Chalcedon (451) to Gregory the Great (590–604).* Part One: "Reception and Contradiction: The Development of the Discussion about Chalcedon from 451 to the Beginning of the Reign of Justinian" (Atlanta: John Knox Press, 1987), 6–10.

11. See Rush, *The Reception of Doctrine* (71–73; 225–29) on Hans Robert Jauss's reception aesthetics and literary hermeneutics, and his retrieval of the Aristotelian notion of *poiesis* ("making" or "creating") in readerly experience, and its appropriation for theology. Similarly, Leonardo Boff writes: "According to an intelligent epistemology, the meaning of a text (setting forth, for example, a rule or some other determination) emerges not only from the minds of the authors of the text (from the *mens patrum,* in the case of a conciliar text) and the words used by these authors (the literal meaning of the text)—but also from the addressees, who are coauthors of the text, inasmuch as it is they who insert the message of the text into the vital contexts in which they find themselves. The addressees, too, place accents, and perceive the relevancy and pertinence of aspects of the

text in question that illuminate or denounce historical situations. The original meaning of the text—the meaning contained in the 'letter'—stirs new echoes when that text is heard in determinate circumstances. The spiritual meaning becomes revealed. To read, then, is always to reread. Whenever we understand, we interpret; this is how our spirit is structured. The original message does not remain a cistern of stagnant water. It becomes a font of living water, ready to generate new meanings, by prolonging and concretizing the original meaning. The latter functions as a generator of new life through the new significations it awakens." See Leonardo Boff, "Theology of Liberation: Creative Acceptance of Vatican II from the Viewpoint of the Poor," in *When Theology Listens to the Poor* (San Francisco: Harper & Row, 1988), 1–31, at 18.

12. Paul Ricoeur, *Interpretation Theory: Discourse and the Surplus of Meaning* (Fort Worth, TX: Texas Christian University Press, 1976).

13. On retrospective meaning, see Francis Schüssler Fiorenza, *Foundational Theology: Jesus and the Church* (New York: Crossroad, 1984), 111–12.

14. On the notion of *loci receptionis,* see Rush, *The Reception of Doctrine,* 325–58.

15. In this sense, the reception of Vatican II is different from that of previous councils like Trent and Vatican I. The significant difference is due precisely to a radical direction set by the Council itself, if Karl Rahner's basic theological interpretation of Vatican II is valid.

16. For a survey of the "effect" (I would prefer "reception") of the Council worldwide, see the range of articles in the section "The Effect of the Council on World Catholicism" in Adrian Hastings, *Modern Catholicism: Vatican II and After* (London: SPCK, 1991).

17. Gilles Routhier, *La Réception d'un Concile* (Paris: Cerf, 1993).

18. Adrian Hastings, "The Council Came to Africa," in *Vatican II: By Those Who Were There,* ed. Alberic Stacpoole (London: G. Chapman, 1986), 315–23.

19. David Pascoe, *Toward a Self-Understanding of a Local Church: The Roman Catholic Church in Australia in the Wake of Vatican II* (STD diss., Weston School of Theology, 1996).

20. Boff, "Creative Acceptance of Vatican II," 8.

21. Segundo Galilea, "Latin America in the Medellín and Puebla Conferences: An Example of Selective and Creative Reception of Vatican II," in *The Reception of Vatican II,* ed. Giuseppe Alberigo, Jean Pierre Jossua, and Joseph A. Komonchak (Washington, DC: Catholic University of America Press, 1987), 59–73.

22. Gustavo Gutiérrez, "The Church and the Poor: A Latin American Perspective," in *The Reception of Vatican II,* ed. Giuseppe Alberigo, Jean Pierre Jossua, and Joseph A. Komonchak (Washington, DC: Catholic University of America Press, 1987), 171–93.

23. Ratzinger and Messori, *The Ratzinger Report,* 29.

24. Two articles in particular present Komonchak's typology of receptions. See J. A. Komonchak, "Interpreting the Second Vatican Council," *Landas: Journal of Loyola School of Theology* 1 (1987): 81–90; Joseph A. Komonchak, "Interpreting the Council: Catholic Attitudes toward Vatican II," in *Being Right: Conservative Catholics in America,* ed. Mary Jo Weaver and R. Scott Appleby (Bloomington: Indiana University Press, 1995), 17–36.

25. Ratzinger, *Principles of Catholic Theology,* 373.

26. Avery Dulles, "The Reception of Vatican II at the Extraordinary Synod of 1985," in *The Reception of Vatican II,* ed. Giuseppe Alberigo, Jean Pierre Jossua, and Joseph A. Komonchak (Washington, DC: Catholic University of America Press, 1987), 349–63.

27. Komonchak, "Thomism and the Second Vatican Council," 73n31.

28. Cardinal Walter Kasper, in reference to his position over against that of Cardinal Joseph Ratzinger regarding the universal/local church, sees the Platonic/Aristotelian typology at work. Walter Kasper, "On the Church: A Friendly Reply to Cardinal Ratzinger," *America* 184 (April 23–30, 2001): 8–14, at 13–14: "When the question of the 'primacy of the churches' is critically examined, it becomes clear that the debate is not about any point of 'Catholic doctrine.' The conflict is between theological opinions and underlying philosophical assumptions. One side [Ratzinger] proceeds by Plato's method; its starting point is the primacy of an idea that is a universal concept. The other side [Kasper] follows Aristotle's approach and sees the universal as existing in a concrete reality. Aristotle's approach, of course, should not be misconstrued as if it were reducing all knowledge to mere empirical data. The medieval controversy between the Platonic and the Aristotelian schools was a debate within the parameters of the common Catholic faith. Thus Bonaventure and Thomas chose different paths in their approach to theological issues, including the matter of the universal authority of the pope. Yet both are revered as doctors of the church; both are honoured as saints. If such a diversity was admitted in the Middle Ages, why should it not be recognized as possible today?" In his subsequent response to Kasper's reply, Ratzinger accepts the Platonic-Aristotelian typology as descriptive of a major difference between Kasper and himself: "The most positive feature of Cardinal Kasper's response to my talk is that he tacitly dropped the reproach from his first article and now assigned to our argument the rank of a 'controversy over a scholastic dispute.' The theses of the ontological and temporal priority of the universal church to individual churches was now treated as a question, 'not of church doctrine, but of theological opinions and of the various related philosophies.' The statement by the Congregation of the Doctrine of the Faith was categorized as my personal theology and tied in with my 'Platonism,' while Kasper traced his own view back to his

more Aristotelian (Thomistic) approach. By reframing the dispute in this way, the question was basically blunted and shifted to another level. The charge was no longer that the Congregation of the Doctrine of the Faith was intent on centralism, restoration and turning the church around. Instead, Cardinal Kasper now noted two different theological points of view separating his theology and mine, which can and perhaps should coexist peacefully." Joseph Ratzinger, "The Local Church and the Universal Church: A Response to Walter Kasper," *America* 185 (November 19, 2001): 7–11, at 8–9. How one envisions the relationship of church and world will in great part depend on what philosophical background theory one is employing, and indeed, on the more basic question of how one envisions the relationship between faith and reason and the relationship between *theology* and *philosophy*.

29. On neo-Augustinianism in the research interests and theological temperament of Ratzinger, see his Joseph Ratzinger, *Milestones: Memoirs 1927–1977* (San Francisco: Ignatius Press, 1998); John L. Allen, *Cardinal Ratzinger: The Vatican's Enforcer of the Faith* (New York: Continuum, 2000); Aidan Nichols, *The Theology of Joseph Ratzinger: An Introductory Study* (Edinburgh: T. & T. Clark, 1988).

30. In a remarkable move, Ratzinger seeks to downplay the significance of the Incarnation as a hermeneutical key for interpreting the best in the tradition and for modeling the relationship of church to world. In a lecture delivered to the *Katholikentag* of 1966 in Bamberg, he rightly shows how belief in the Incarnation was a later development in christology, postdating an earlier eschatologically oriented christology. He goes on to show how in the Middle Ages there was a shift away from an "Incarnation-oriented Christianity" to "the eschatological phase," emphasizing both the cross and the future-orientation of Christian faith. After remarking on the "naïve optimism" of John XXIII and then of the Council, he speaks of the debate between these two christologies during the latter sessions of the Council as "the first blow in the battle for

Christian spirituality in our modern world." Ratzinger, "Catholicism After the Council," 15–18.

31. On the theology of Chenu, see Christophe F. Potworowski, *Contemplation and Incarnation: The Theology of Marie-Dominique Chenu* (Montreal: McGill-Queen's University Press, 2001).

32. Kasper, "The Continuing Challenge of the Second Vatican Council," 171: "As in the case of every council, the theoretical mediation of these [juxtaposed] positions is a task for the theology that comes afterwards."

33. Pottmeyer, "A New Phase in the Reception of Vatican II," 39.

34. See Ormond Rush, "Determining Catholic Orthodoxy: Monologue or Dialogue?" *Pacifica* 12 (1999): 123–42; Wolfgang Beinert, "Theologische Erkenntnislehre," in *Glaubenszugänge: Lehrbuch der Katholischen Dogmatik,* vol. I, ed. Wolfgang Beinert, I (Paderborn: Ferdinand Schöningh, 1995), 47–197.

35. Komonchak, "Vatican II as an 'Event.'"

36. See Kuncheria Pathil, *Models in Ecumenical Dialogue: A Study of the Methodological Development in the Commission on "Faith and Order" of the World Council of Churches* (Bangalore: Dharmaram Publications, 1981); Peter Bouteneff and Dagmar Heller, eds., *Interpreting Together: Essays in Hermeneutics* (Geneva: WCC Publications, 2001); G. R. Evans, *Methods in Ecumenical Theology: The Lessons So Far* (Cambridge: Cambridge University Press, 1996).

Chapter 4

1. Luis Alonso Schökel and José María Bravo, *A Manual of Hermeneutics,* trans. Brook W. R. Pearson (New York/Sheffield, UK: Sheffield Academic Press, 1998), 170.

2. Congar, *Tradition and Traditions: An Historical and a Theological Essay,* 127: "The texts that speak of the 'inspiration' of the councils are without number. Even before Nicaea, and in reference to the information given by the New Testament itself, the councils had expressed their awareness that they were working with the Holy Spirit present and active among them." Congar goes on to note that it was this constant guidance by the Holy Spirit that was regarded as guaranteeing *continuity* with the past: "It follows that the work of manifestation or revelation of himself and his plan, which God initiated through the prophets, and then accomplished in Jesus Christ, to whom we have access through the witness of the apostles—this manifestation continues in the Church, through the action of the Holy Spirit. I have already briefly demonstrated how St Thomas, for example, saw this continuity, while distinguishing within it different qualitative levels. I note here some more expressions of this awareness of continuity in the manifestation of the truth of salvation, as this is realized, according to the requirements of each particular age, during the course of the Church's history, under the action of the Holy Spirit 'revealing' the intention of God, and 'inspiring' for this the Fathers, councils, canons, and the major events of the life of the Church....Between the time of the Church and the time of the prophets, of Christ and of the apostles, there exists a far-reaching continuity by reason of the fact that a single principle is active, working towards a single, unique term: the Holy Spirit" (131, 137).

3. Correlating *DV,* 12, and *LG,* 12, it is the *universitas fidelium* (the whole body of the faithful—not just the magisterium) who are the *ecclesia* receiving and interpreting scripture.

4. de la Potterie, "Interpretation of Holy Scripture," 238–46.

5. Pottmeyer likewise asserts that the term "the council's spirit" is to be understood pneumatologically, and that this demands an interpretative approach to the Council and its texts akin to "discernment of spirits" *(discretio spirituum).* See Pottmeyer, "A New Phase in the Reception of Vatican II," 41–43.

6. Quoted in Ibid., 35.

7. Concerning the order of the authorities mentioned in *DV,* 8, Walter Kasper observes: "It is no accident that the magisterium is only mentioned in third place. The ecclesiality of faith is not exhausted by an attitude of obedience to the Church's teaching authority. That authority is situated within the community of believers and under the authority of the word of revelation. It is not a super-criterion ruling over the Church and its common search for truth in lonely Olympian majesty and issuing condemnations." Walter Kasper, *An Introduction to Christian Faith* (London: Burns & Oates, 1980), 146–47. See further, Rush, "Determining Catholic Orthodoxy: Monologue or Dialogue?" 131–36.

8. With regard to the content of the conciliar teaching, the Council only slowly came to incorporating a broader pneumatology into its vision. See Yves Congar, "The Pneumatology of Vatican II," in *I Believe in the Holy Spirit* (New York: Crossroad, 1997), 167–73. The first part of this book, referred to here, was published separately as *The Holy Spirit in the "Economy": Revelation and Experience of the Spirit.*

9. Ibid., 172.

10. O'Malley, "Reform, Historical Consciousness, and Vatican II's *Aggiornamento,*" 66–73.

11. "Pope John's Opening Speech at the Council," in Walter Abbott, ed., *The Documents of Vatican II* (London: Geoffrey Chapman, 1966), 710–19, at 715.

12. O'Malley, "Reform, Historical Consciousness, and Vatican II's *Aggiornamento,*" 73. Within that conservative agenda, different ways of dealing with newness are allowed: "We can list…five reform procedures which such styles of thinking allow: (1) reform by excision or suppression (keep what you have by removing threats to it); (2) reform by addition or accretion (keep what you have untouched, but add new things alongside it); (3) reform by revival (keep what you have by breathing new life into it); (4) reform by accommodation

(keep what you have by making adjustments for differences in times and places); (5) reform by development (keep what you have, but let it expand and mature to its final perfection)."

13. Komonchak, "Riflessioni storiografiche sul Vaticano II come evento," and its further development in Komonchak, "Vatican II as an 'Event.'"

14. Cf. *Catechism of the Catholic Church,* 1099, which speaks of the Holy Spirit as the church's living memory.

15. See Yves Congar, "The Conciliar Structure or Regime of the Church," *Concilium* 167 (1983): 3–9; Yves Congar, "The Council as an Assembly and the Church as Essentially Conciliar," in *One, Holy, Catholic, and Apostolic: Studies in the Nature and Role of the Church in the Modern World,* ed. Herbert Vorgrimler (London: Sheed and Ward, 1968), 44–88; Margaret O'Gara and Michael Vertin, "The Holy Spirit's Assistance to the Magisterium in Teaching: Theological and Philosophical Issues," *Catholic Theological Society of America Proceedings* 51 (1996): 125–42; John Zizioulas, "The Development of Conciliar Structures to the Time of the First Ecumenical Council," in *Councils and the Ecumenical Movement* (Geneva: World Council of Churches, 1968), 34–51; Wolfgang Beinert, "Konziliarität der Kirche: Ein Beitrag zur ökumenischen Epistemologie," in *Vom Finden und Verkünden der Wahrheit in der Kirche: Beiträge zur theologischen Erkenntnislehre* (Freiburg: Herder, 1993), 325–50. See further the articles in Gebhard Fürst, ed., *Dialog als Selbstvollzug der Kirche* (Freiburg: Herder, 1997).

16. O'Malley, "Reform, Historical Consciousness, and Vatican II's *Aggiornamento,*" 76, 77.

17. Matt 16:3; Luke 12:56.

18. See Rino Fisichella, "Signs of the Times," in *Dictionary of Fundamental Theology,* ed. René Latourelle and Rino Fisichella (Slough, UK: ST PAULS; New York: Crossroad Publishing Company, 1994), 995–1001.

19. *LG,* 12. See Rush, "The Offices of Christ."

20. John Paul II, *Novo Millennio Ineunte. Apostolic Letter of John Paul II* (Strathfield, Australia: St. Paul's Publications, 2001), pp. 58 and 56.

21. Quoted in Xavier Rynne, *Vatican Council II* (Maryknoll, NY: Orbis Books, 2002), 222.

INDEX

Teilhard de Chardin, Pierre, 11

theologians, 8–12, 65, 71, 76

theological anthropology, 15, 17, 78

theological epistemology, 63, 65f, 67

Thomas Aquinas, 14, 15, 16, 61

Thomism, 10, 14–16, 15f, 61f, 64; and Augustinianism, 15f, 60–63, 64f

threefold offices of Christ, 21f, 82f

Tillard, Jean-Marie, 53

tradition, living, 4, 5, 43; the whole, 4–7

Trent, Council of, 13

Tübingen School, 11

unanimity, 27f

Unitatis redintegratio, 22, 27

Vatican I, 13, 27, 39; and Vatican II, x, 13

weight, authoritative, 32f

world: behind the text, 1–34, 49; in front of the text, 52–68; of the text, 35–51

world-church, 24, 25, 53